Christian
Time
Management

Christian Time Management

Investing God's Gift Wisely

Kenneth A. Erickson

Publishing House
St. Louis

Scripture quotations marked TEV are from the Good News Bible, the Bible in *Today's English Version.* Copyright © American Bible Society 1966, 1971, 1976.

Copyright 1985 by Concordia Publishing House
3558 South Jefferson Ave., St. Louis, MO 63118
Manufactured in the United States of America

Library of Congress Cataloging in Publication Data

Erickson, Kenneth A.
    Christian time management.

    1. Time management   Religious aspects   Christianity.
I. Title.
BV4598.5.E74   1985   640'.43'0242   84-23866
ISBN 0-570-03972-X (pbk.)

---

1 2 3 4 5 6 7 8 9 10   MAL   94 93 92 91 90 89 88 87 86 85

Contents _____

Foreword		7
Acknowledgments		9
Introduction		11
1.	Timewasters	13
2.	Interruptions, Interruptions	17
3.	Identifying Goals and Objectives	24
4.	"Can't Say No" Syndrome	33
5.	Procrastination, the Great Putoff	37
6.	Planning and Prioritizing	44
7.	Effective Verbal Communication	53
8.	Nonverbal Communication	63
9.	Written Communication	70
10.	Meetings Are Too Long	74
11.	Telephone: Servant or Master?	80
12.	Problem Solving and Decision Making	85
13.	Delegation: Key to Saving Time	92
14.	Secretaries: Leadership Team Members	99
15.	Volunteer Programs	105
16.	Appreciation and Praise	114
17.	Summary	119

Foreword _____

This book is the result of years of wrestling with time-management problems I worked as an industrial personnel director, a city high school principal, and a superintendent of schools. Only after becoming a university professor did I take time to analyze my hectic work pace in each previous position and begin a search for improved time-management practices.

Effective time management developed into one of my primary investigations. As a result of this study I have presented time-management seminars to persons in nearly all vocations in many states and several countries overseas.

I have a special empathy for the problems many Christian leaders face with their daily time-management challenges. While this book focuses on their needs, it is of equal value for that vast number of lay volunteers seeking to serve God in a wide range of responsibilities, from council presidents to chairpersons of various committees. Many volunteers often are employed full time in the work world or at home—beset by time challenges similar to those in full-time church service. The more time-effective volunteers become in their daily work, the more time they can dedicate to serving God as His light of the world and His salt of the earth.

Acknowledgments

A number of persons have offered helpful suggestions following seminar attendance or have reviewed drafts of chapters for this book. I am very thankful to Pastors Roy D. Brewer, John L. Casteel, Clyde Everton, Dan B. Hallgrimson, Jack D. Hodges, Rod J. W. Johnson, Terry A. Moe, and Elmer G. Steenbock for their special assistance.

I am indebted to some of my former work associates from whom I also learned about effective time management. Verne A. Duncan, James J. Fenwick, Walter H. Gmelch, and Robert "Ozzie" Rose have been some of my best teachers.

Don Bowman and his capable staff at Endeavors for Excellence have been most competent in planning and scheduling time management seminars. Linda Gill's positive attitude and competent work have eliminated the normal distress of manuscript typing.

Most of all I express my continuing love and appreciation to my wife, Lois, who has demonstrated effective time management skills while meeting the needs of four children and a husband. In addition to her regular reviews of the manuscript and her constructive suggestions, I have found her constant encouragement and support invaluable.

Introduction ___

"Sometimes I think there are as many demands on my time as there are members in the organization," a Christian leader observed. Feeling overcome by his countless responsibilities, he concluded, "There never is enough time to do everything that everyone else wants me to do."

A survey of managers revealed that 99 percent claimed they had insufficient time to do their work. Most also stated they would need 50 percent more time to complete their responsibilites. Any leader experiencing time management problems is not alone.

Time is not a typical resource. It can't be stored for future use. Neither can we borrow on tomorrow's time for use today. The only way we deal with time is to spend it. Our choice is whether to treat time carelessly as if it were cheap or to value time by spending it as effectively as possible.

Christian leaders face the challenge of juggling a myriad of demands on their fragmented time. They can never really say, "I've caught up with my work." A contractor finishes construction and can see the completed building. An attorney wins or loses a case and knows the outcome. No church leader, however, can physically weigh, count, or measure spiritual results.

Improvement in use of time is strictly a personal matter. No one can accomplish it for another. Yet effort invested in learning a more effective use of time can add to the achievement of an organization's goals, heighten personal satisfactions, reduce the anxieties of daily pressures, offer increased time for planning and studying, as well as allow more time for family relationships. Effort invested in improving one's use of time pays dividends.

1. Timewasters____

Pastor Mark arrived at his office at 8:30. Last night's board meeting had dragged on past 11:00. He resolved that today he would tackle the overdue annual report for regional headquarters.

Martha, the nursery school supervisor, was waiting for him. She wanted to know about a board member's complaint of her children's "abuse of facilities."

As she left, the architect phoned. "When will your building committee know the storage space needed in our remodeling plans?" he appealed.

When Mark finally had time to pick up the annual report forms, he stopped to glance at the mail at the same time. A letter on top alleged a loose handrail on the front steps was a "hazard for the elderly." Mark dropped the letter and started out to inspect the railing. A young woman stopped him in the hallway. "I am here in response to a request for temporary secretarial help," she commented. Mark invited her into his office for an interview.

After she left, Mark wondered, "Will I ever find time for the report?" He was picking up the papers again when Debbie, his secretary, interrupted him. "Things have been so hectic lately we haven't been able to discuss our top-priority projects. I spent this morning on the choir music order and now find the council didn't approve the purchase." The phone intruded on their discussion. The library committee Chair sounded disturbed. Had the board really cut their book budget by 33 percent? Mark promised to get back to her about the problem tomorrow.

He glanced at his watch. Already late for his service club luncheon, he rushed out the door forgetting to tell Debbie he had a finance committee meeting after lunch. When Mark finally returned to the office, three people were waiting to see him—a second applicant, a local heating company representative, and the ladies' auxiliary president—five phone calls were to be made. During the third of his conferences Debbie waved good-bye from the hallway and left for home.

Another day down the tube with the annual report still on his desk. Is it inevitable that time demands of others always absorb the entire day? Couldn't Mark achieve control of some part of his time each day?

We can empathize with Mark. We've all had similar days. When we analyze our failure to control time, we realize how often we fail to plan, fail to delegate, procrastinate, and have trouble saying no. We can appreciate Pogo's philosophy when he said, "We have met the enemy and he is us."

Some timewasters are obvious, some more subtle. I have categorized typical timewasters under two headings— "Conspicuous Timewasters" and "Inconspicuous Timewasters." Normally we overlook the latter, though they may be equally harmful.

Conspicuous Timewasters

1. Permitting telephone interruptions at any time.
2. Allowing unscheduled drop-in visitors to appropriate time.
3. Maintaining a continual open-door policy.
4. Participating in long and poorly planned meetings, scheduled or unscheduled.
5. Responding readily to each emergency crisis.
6. Keeping associates ignorant by failing to share significant information—confusing them with garbled communication.
7. Failing as a listener to verify what was heard by testing it with feedback.
8. Yielding to the "yes obsession"—fearing to say no. Forgetting there never is enough time to do everything that everyone else wants a leader to do.
9. Working with a lake of paper flooding my desk.
10. Attempting to do too many tasks at once; finding it difficult to complete any of them.
11. Failing to question nonfunctional office layouts that encourge visual distractions or traffic intrusions.

12. Consenting to extend coffee breaks and prolonged lunch periods.

Inconspicuous Timewasters

13. Lacking a clear understanding of the leader's role and most important responsibilities.
14. Working without annual organizational goals and monthly objectives.
15. Failing to plan, prioritize, and schedule one's daily work.
16. Specializing in less important but more enjoyable functions. Majoring in the minors.
17. Refusing to trust paid or volunteer co-workers by failing to delegate significant responsibilities. Allowing "upbucking" or upward delegation to overload a leader's workday.
18. Losing potential assistance from the secretary or other co-workers by not considering them important members of the leadership team.
19. Spending time on the routine, less-difficult aspects of the work. Leaders seldom recognize this as a timewaster, although secretaries rank it as one of their bosses' top-five timewasters.
20. Remaining so indispensable to staff members they become dependent and lose initiative.
21. Being a perfectionist, fearing mistakes, and functioning as a bottleneck to task completion.
22. Procrastinating work on difficult or distasteful projects.
23. Participating in fruitless conferencing where problems are rehashed with no conclusions as to who will take what action.
24. Disappearing with no notice as to where the leader has gone, if he is coming back, and if so, when. This is the lost-leader syndrome, which leaves co-workers embarrassingly ignorant.
25. Realizing the amount of time required to complete tasks—having unrealistically high self-expectations.
26. Diminishing worker satisfaction and productivity by neglecting to recognize each person's achievements.
27. Hiring inadequate personnel. Disregarding the importance of extremely thorough employment practices.

Summary

Regardless of the timewasters that plague us as leaders, old habit patterns die hard. Ingrained practices serve as internal flywheels. They are difficult to brake. Improvements desired must be identified and practiced faithfully. Allowing even minor exceptions will sabotage our progress toward desired goals. Once in place, however, improved time habits will continue to work in our behalf.

The next chapter considers one of the most destructive timewasters to plague leaders—interruptions.

2. *Interruptions, Interruptions*

Many complain that their leadership position is monopolized by a series of interruptions interrupted by interruptions. Attempting to resolve this dilemma can seem as futile as putting beads on a string with no knot on the end.

The typical leader is interrupted on the average of every eight minutes during the day. Yet, as former President Eisenhower observed on retirement, most items that are important are seldom urgent while those that appear urgent are seldom important.

It is easy for leaders to assume that all crises faced are an unavoidable part of the job. This is only partially true. Unique crises usually are unavoidable, but these represent a minority of the intrusions. Many leaders treat all interruptions as if they were equally important and equally beyond control. This is not true. The majority of intrusions are relatively unimportant and subject to greater control.

Do I Need to Be Needed?

Some leaders get a tremendous satisfaction out of jumping from crisis to crisis. They feel most stimulated when living in the eye of a storm. Such persons may even help create crises by failing to share information, failing to plan, or failing to delegate. They tend to be "adrenalin addicts" who thrive on a consistent series of intrusions. Unfortunately they often shortchange their primary responsibilities, as they have little time to move toward organizational goals and objectives.

This compulsion for action is aggravated if a leader feels personally indispenable. Continual availabitity to anyone about anything appears to be such a leader's top priority. Is it possible that some of us feel more important if there are more interruptions?

An open-door policy may be one evidence of the always-available philosophy. Some leaders claim improved communication results from the always-open door. But they increase the wrong type of communication—that which is trivial or social in nature. A leader can better be accessible through an advance calendar appointment. That does not require a door that functions as a freeway—an inviting portal where anyone can enter or stand until recognized. There seems to be an unwritten agreement that achieving eye contact not only legitimizes an interruption—it guarantees a visit. Many times I have been sitting at my desk deep in thought. Somehow I sensed a presence and looked up. There was a head protuding around my office door. Even a faint smile of recognition on my part encouraged a body to follow the head into my office and plop down in a chair. Fifteen minutes were easily lost—plus the time needed to regain momentum on the interrupted project.

If everyone is allowed to control how we spend our time, it will be difficult for us to remain faithful to the church's mission. Salespersons, special-interest advocates, and a host of drop-ins will continually demand our time and disrupt our ability to concentrate on our primary purposes.

The attentive and always-available leader must ask these searching questions:
1. Do I need to be needed?
2. Do I seek to earn the goodwill of others by continually being available.
3. How much goodwill can our organization afford?

Interruptions, an Illusion of Legitimacy

Most interruptions *appear* legitimate. The open door looks friendly. The incoming phone calls sound important. Yet the *assumption* that all are significant disrupts attention needed for more important responsibilities. A leader loses work momentum if an interruption shatters the train of thought. Progress halts. If the intrusion involves emotional empathy, the former task may become dead in its tracks. Starting it again requires extra effort. Like a stalled automobile, more energy is required to get it moving than to keep it moving. We face similar challenges each time we accept intrusions. Eventually frustrations rise, energy drains away, and valuable time is forever gone.

Realistically, we cannot eliminate all interruptions. Yet we tend to be lax in dealing with intrusions. While busily dictating at my desk I have been asked by an intruder, "Are you busy?" If I replied, "What can I do for you?" I was guilty of legitimizing an ill-mannered interruption. I finally learned that whenever I fail to protect my own planning time, intrusions continue to run my life. Leaders either must control interruptions or relinquish the possibility of achieving their most important objectives.

This chapter seeks to help leaders reduce both the frequency and the length of intrusions on their time. One evaluative technique is to ask the question, "What interruptions would I miss if they never happened?" This may give some insight into one's tendency to welcome interruptions.

Why Leaders Self-Interrupt

The more difficult the task at hand the greater the temptation for us to self-interrupt. It is easy to self-distract by picking up an impulse job. Temptations include, "I must call Fred," or worse yet, "I must go and see Fred." A higher-priority task has been self-interrupted.

I also learned that with a desk top full of paper my eyes help seek relief from a difficult job by shifting my attention else-where—a phone call to return, a letter to write, an article to examine, or the incoming mail to read. A clear desk, except for the one most important project, is the best way to start each day.

Analyzing Interruption Patterns

Gathering some data is the first step toward understanding the scope and seriousness of this problem. Concerned leaders are encouraged to keep a visitors' log for a week. This should include the names of those involved, the length of the visit, the topic, and whether or not the contact was prescheduled or a drop-in.

One discovery probably will be that about 20 percent of your contacts are responsible for 80 percent of your interruptions. If the majority come from paid or volunteer co-workers, a communication problem may exist. If leaders fail to share important information when delegating, they will spend extra time later answering questions and making corrections.

An analysis of interruption causes should include the following questions:

1. What is my interruption expectancy level?
2. How much quiet time can I tolerate before I become uncomfortable enough to self-interrupt or welcome an intrusion?
3. Has my desire to help individuals driven me to be uncomfortable if others leave me alone too long?
4. Have I been lured by an egocentric attitude to think that the more I am interrupted, the more important I must be?

Suggestions for Coping with Interruptions

Leaders must learn to live with but limit the length of interruptions beyond their control. The majority of recurring intrusions can be controlled.

1. Effective time management is a matter of both planned availability and planned unavailability. Set aside "reception time," when you are available for unscheduled or drop-in conferences. Also set aside some quiet or concentration time each day (one hour minimum) for planning or preparation, when you take no calls and see no visitors except in real emergencies. Place your own name on the calendar for that hour.
2. Periodically review your organization's objectives. Discuss current priorities with paid and volunteer co-workers. Reduce their need to pursue you with questions due to lack of information.
3. Request that the person scheduling your appointments write down the topic and anticipated visit length. Also ask that she phone you when the time is up. While you may not be sure how long a discussion may take, you remain in control as you reply, "We're discussing an important item and don't wish to

be disturbed," or, "We'll be only another three minutes," or you can ask the visitor, "How much more time do you think we will need?"

4. With an unscheduled drop-in, suggest that the two of you agree on another meeting time when you can be better prepared. If you choose to handle the matter immediately, explain that "it's good to see you and I'd like to chat, but I have only a few minutes before my next responsibility."

5. With a salesman or similar drop-in, remain standing as he enters the office. Once a visitor is seated, it is more difficult to get the person out of a chair. Ask him to outline briefly what he wishes to talk about so you can let him know if you wish to discuss it further. Some leaders have just one visitor's chair in the office and leave books on it which can be removed when inviting someone to stay for a while.

6. If someone on the phone fails to get to the point, say in a kind but firm manner, "I want to help you but I do have some other responsibilities waiting. Would you assist me by suggesting specifically how I might help you?"

7. When you are very busy and someone drops by and asks, "May I see you for a minute?" you can reply, "I'm rushed now. Unless it's a real emergency, please check with me later."

8. Should a coworker repeatedly come to you with questions, request that he accumulate a number of items and then go over them all at one time. Analyze whether you should delegate more authority to such persons.

9. Be skilled in terminating conferences or interviews. Use courteous clues to end your discussion, such as, "Does that take care of our business?" or, "Is there anything else we should discuss?"

10. To curtail visual interruptions, turn your desk so your back is to the office door or major traffic areas.

11. Develop a system of well-communicated cues to control intrusions. One leader hung a circle next to his office door. With the green side out, drop-ins were welcome. With the red side out, drop-ins were to avoid interrupting and talk with the secretary. Many interruptions persist because leaders fail to

notify co-workers when they need to be left alone.

12. Determine the purpose of a person's visit within the first minute. Then focus on achieving that purpose. Avoid becoming sidetracked.

13. If visitors or callers on the phone have little terminal facility, suggest that they put their concern in writing with a recommended solution before you further review the matter.

14. Group your return phone calls. Consider making them at 11:30 a.m. Recipients will be less inclined to ramble just before lunch. Allow time for essential discussion but not for chatter.

15. If a person is late for an appointment, share your resulting time constraints. Ask if the business can be accomplished within the limited time now available or if the appointment should be rescheduled. Being considerate to one late person may make you rude to all those who follow.

16. Go to another person's work area rather than asking the person to come to yours. You can leave another office more easily than you can get someone to leave your office.

17. If you have a secretary, ask her to screen all drop-in visitors. When asked if you are busy, she may reply, "Yes, but if it is an emergency, I'll interrupt. Otherwise, may I call you when he is free?"

18. Whenever you must work an extended day, go to work early rather than staying late. Poet William Stafford tells of his practice of getting up early to write. "You can usually be free most of the time if you wake up before other people." An early morning hour can be the most productive segment of your day.

19. Request that when making appointments your secretary record the agenda topic on your calendar so you can be prepared for the discussion. This discourages the casual drop-in with no special business to discuss.

20. When business with a visitor is completed, get up from your desk and thank the person for coming in. This signals the end of the conversation.

21. Locate an alternative work area or hideway unknown to drop-ins where you can work in privacy whenever necessary.

22. Diagnose the problem by collecting information on drop-in and telephone interruptions. Record the person's name, length of time, and purpose of the contact. Analysis of the data will furnish ideas for some procedural improvements.

Summary

Leaders will never be free of all interruptions. Yet effective leaders can cut interruption time in half by adopting some of the suggestions above. Quickly getting to the point and refusing to dwell on small talk will save far more time than we realize.

Productive leaders also strive to make co-workers independent in their work. No leader should need to be continually accessible to paid or volunteer associates. The competent leader delegates responsibility and authority, expects others to do their tasks, and increasingly has less need to be needed.

We tend to concentrate on the interruptions others inflict on us and overlook those we force upon others. Jesus reminds us to "always treat others as you would like them to treat you" (Matthew 7:12 NEB). Concerned leaders should attempt to set an example for co-workers as some of our best learnings are caught, not taught.

Simply stated, the able leader regains control of much of the time previously usurped by others. Competent leaders understand that they must either control the majority of their time or allow others to exploit their time, drain their energies, compound their stress, and divert them from their organization's major mission.

3. *Identifying Goals and Objectives* _____

*The gift of life and the freedom
to live it as we wish
is life's awesome responsibility.
(John Lloyd Ogilvie)*

The board members faced a tough decision. They had to reduce the school district's total operating budget by 10 percent. As superintendent, I was to recommend where they make the specific program cuts.

Advice from staff members was abundant. Their initial reaction was, "I realize you must cut somewhere, but our department can't survive more reductions!" They added convincing arguments on the importance of their specialty to the welfare of students.

A second wave of advice was based on the realization that program reductions were inevitable. The easiest way, I was counseled, was to reduce funding 10 percent to every activity regardless of its functions. On the surface this appeared equitable. It would result in the least resentment.

Some of us were uneasy with an easy approach. Conceivably we should *increase* funding to more essential programs and decrease others by more than 10 percent. But how would we decide? Our district had no written goals to serve as yardsticks. We felt like a football team scheduled to play on a field with no yard markers or goalposts.

I shared my dilemma with the school board. For years our schools basically had been repeating what they had done the previous year. We had added new programs but we had deleted little from our offerings. Recent additions included girls' athletics, expanded health programs, education for handicapped, family life education, computer education, and additional languages such as Chinese and Arabic. Recommending an across-the-board program reduction would be educationally unsound.

I asked the board to appoint a citizens' task force of our community's best minds to define goals for public education today. In addition, I appointed several educators as resource persons to be available at the study group's request.

The task force's first responsibility was to list all educational expectations that citizens had for their public schools. Next they were to rank these functions in priority order from the most to the least important. Finally, they were to divide the prioritized list into three categories:

1. High priority functions for which the schools were funded and would be held responsible to the public
2. Important functions for which the schools were not funded and therefore would not be responsible
3. Functions not considered the responsibility of public schools

Faculties studied the final task force report. They suggested minor revisions. Then the school board reviewed and adopted the document on educational goals and objectives. Finally, we had a yardstick against which to evalute the relative importance of the school district's various functions, which too often had been justified by the cliche, "We've always done it that way!"

Goals and Objectives as Timesavers

Regardless of our specific responsibilities, each of us spends all of our 168 hours a week. Whether we spend them prudently or waste them depends largely on whether we have clear goals and objectives. *Doing the job right* (efficiently) is not enough. *Doing the right job right* (effectively) suggests movement toward preselected targets. Leaders experience difficulties when they confuse efficiency with effectiveness. Becoming efficient does not make us effective. For example, we may be efficiently doing low-priority tasks that are a waste of time. Periodically, organizations need to refocus on their mission—to review their objectives and identify functions they should add or drop. This protects conscientious leaders from wasting time on less-important objectives.

Discrepancies Regarding Goals and Objectives

One management authority claims that objectives which workers set for themselves seldom are what the leader thinks they should be. In fact, a capable worker's perception of his responsibilities varies more from the leader's concept than that of a less able worker.

Another study revealed that the average worker's opinion of his or her job duties will vary 25 to 30 percent from the leader's thinking. This predestines the worker to a substantial performance deficiency even with no mistakes. Most organizations tend to drift off target when leaders fail to define and clearly communicate major orgnaizational goals to work associates.

Too Many Objectives are Self-Defeating

Competent organizational leaders normally limit their number of major objectives. At any one time they will identify no more than three to five. Working with long "to do" lists of unprioritized objectives is not productive. With no prioritization of targets, leaders tend to specialize in vocational hobbies—favorite activities they find comfortable and personally rewarding. With a long cafeteria-type menu of objectives, it is tempting to choose the more enjoyable activities and neglect the higher-priority but less-satisfying functions.

Setting Goals, Objectives, and Targets

Goal setting is a fundamental skill of effective leaders. Without this skill there is little coordination of an organization's efforts. The attainment of an organization mission follows the establishment of annual goals, 90-day objectives, and weekly targets.

Identifying goals and objectives does take time. Yet it is an *investment* from which leaders earn a significant return.

26

Organizational objectives should be
1. specific
2. in writing
3. stated in terms of outcomes desired
4. easily understood
5. attainable within a reasonable length of time
6. supported by a time schedule when dealing with major tasks
7. clearly understood by the leader and all co-workers
8. reviewed periodically to determine progress and to make revisions when needed

Establishing Congregational Goals

A church congregation failing to identify and focus on its mission, goals, and prioritized objectives can drift like a ship without a rudder. Governing boards should help develop these goals in cooperation with congregational members.

The material which follows comes from the *Congregational Goals Handbook,* prepared by Kenneth Erickson and Stuart Young. It is modeled after an educational goals program developed by Phi Delta Kappa Commission of Educational Planning. The original document has been effectively used by many school districts throughout the United States.

There are a number of advantages in this goal identification and prioritization process:

1. All congregational members can be actively involved at an appropriate level. The procedure requires only a moderate investment of parishioner time.
2. It provides for rapid collection and analysis of data that is easily understandable to congregational members.
3. The system furnishes information with which to develop prioritized goals. If repeated at a later date, it highlights any changes in a congregation's perceived mission.
4. It includes a second instrument which determines how well current congregational programs are meeting the goals identified.
5. The goal development process adapts easily to congregations of any size. Local leaders can plan and supervise the program without external assistance.

Table I

Prioritized Congregational Goals. Average score is shown in Column "B" (with 5 being high). The rank order of each goal in Column "A" is recorded in Column "C."

A	B	C
Congregational Goals _____ Church Eugene, Oregon November 19 ____	Average Score of Ten Small Groups	Priority Rank Order
Encourage open discussion of church problems as they arise.	3.6	4
Provide fellowship opportunities (socials, coffee hours, etc.).	.7	17
Provide some variety in worship experiences (e.g., Sunday evening worship, guest speakers, old familiar hymns, junior worship service).	3.3	7
Be aware of and minister to the needs of the pastor.	2.9	9
Reach out to the community . . . visit the lonely, shut-ins, sick, etc.	3.5	5
Provide special program(s) to meet needs of the high school youth.	4.0	2
Share the good news of God's love in our own neighborhood.	2.5	11
Keep members informed of activities of the church at large.	.6	18
Accept, visit and support each other with genuine warmth . . . help everyone realize their own self-worth.	4.1	1
Establish cottage or small-group activities within the congregation.	.8	16
Give personal support to early communicants and catechumens.	3.2	8
Each member of the congregation serves as a minister in the home and on the job.	1.3	14
Provide an effective teaching ministry which helps entire family to grow in its faith.	3.7	3

Increase awareness and support of church missions.	.9	15
Communicate daily with God through the study of His Word and through prayer.	2.8	10
Give regularly and sacrificially of income for God's work . . . give of myself (time, talents, energy) in God's service.	3.4	6
Provide worship and fellowship opportunities with Christians outside our congregation.	1.6	12
Train members for evangelism . . . how to express a personal faith to another person.	1.4	13

Procedure for Ranking Congregational Goals

The congregation's governing board appoints a Goals Task Force to establish local goals. All congregational members are invited to propose goals they feel important for task force consideration. Following that, the task force may choose one of the following alternatives:

1. Develop its own original list of goals,
2. Modify a previously established list of congregational goals (such as those shown in Section "A" of Table I),
3. Adopt a prepared list of goal statements similar to those on Table I if they are a "good fit" for the local congregation.

The following steps are typical of a congregational goal-setting meeting.

1. Each member individually prioritizes the prepared list of congregational goals.
2. Members are assigned to groups of four to seek small-group consensus on a ranking of the goals. (These discussions are one of the most valuable activities of the entire process.)
3. Small groups turn in their prioritized lists of church goals.
4. Assistants tally the small-group results and prepare a master ranking of congregational goals based on these deliberations. The results of one congregation's work are shown in Columns "B" and "C" of Table I.

It is unlikely that various congregations would develop identical lists of prioritized goals. (The results shown represent the

Table II

Rating of Congregational Performance Levels. How well do current congregational programs meet each of the prioritized goals identified?

Group _____ Congregation _____

	Not a Responsibility	Extremely Poor	Inadequate	Fair but More Needs to be Done	Good—Leave as Is	Too Much Is Being Done
	0	1	2	3	4	5

A	B	C
Where Most Work Needed	**Goals**	**Rank Score**
7	Encourage open discussion of church problems as they arise.	1.7
18	Provide fellowship opportunities (socials, coffee hours, etc.).	4.7
6	Provide some variety in worship experiences (e.g., Sunday evening worship, guest speakers, old familiar hymns, junior worship service).	1.5
15	Be aware of and minister to the needs of the pastor	3.2
5	Reach out to the community . . . visit the lonely, shut-ins, sick, etc.	1.4
8	Provide special program(s) to meet needs of the high school youth	1.75
3	Share the good news of God's love in our own neighborhood	1.15
13	Keep members informed of activities of the church at large	2.7
16	Accept, visit, and support each other with genuine warmth . . . help everyone realize their own self-worth	3.6
10	Establish cottage or small-group activities within the congregation.	2.1
17	Give personal support to early communicants and catechumens	4.1

4	Each member of the congregation serves as a minister in the home and on the job.	1.2
11	Provide an effective teaching ministry which helps entire family to grow in its faith.	2.2
12	Increase awareness and support of church missions	2.5
14	Communicate daily with God through the study of His Word and through prayer.	2.8
9	Give regularly and sacrificially of income for God's work . . . give of myself (time, talents, energy) in God's service.	1.9
2	Provide worship and fellowship opportunities with Christians outside our congregation.	.9
1	Train members for evangelism . . . how to express a personal faith to another person.	.85

thinking of members of one congregation in Oregon.) There is no assurance that goals ranked higher actually are the most important. The results could indicate instead that adequate emphasis has been lacking in certain essential areas which now call for increased attention.

Procedure for Evaluating Congregational Needs

At a second meeting, congregational members rate how well they think their church meets each goal identified. Members complete a form similar to that shown on the top of Table II.

Individual members each read the goal statements and ask, "In my opinion, how well are current congregational programs meeting this goal?" Assistants tally and average all responses as shown in Column "C" of Table II. These figures in Column "C" are the basis of the ranking in Column "A," which show where the most congregational work is apparently needed.

In the example shown, congregational members chose "Train members for evangelism . . . and how to express a personal faith to another person" as the goal needing most attention. At the other extreme, they felt least emphasis was needed in "Provide fellowship opportunities (socials, coffee hours, etc.)."

Summary

In his New Year's Day sermon our pastor stated that each of us had just received 12 crisp, clean pages—one for each month of the year. Each page had from 28 to 31 empty squares which would be filled with activities by year's end. I pondered, "What activities will crowd my calendar during the year? Who will determine the activities that appropriate my time? Will my time-consumers match my most important goals and objectives? What percent of my time will have been consumed by low-priority activities and interruptions?"

Leaders seldom *find* time for setting goals and objectives. Each must *reallocate* some of the time now expended on less-significant activities. Establishing goals and objectives can be a giant step toward the more effective use of time. Prioritized goals pinpoint our most important responsibilities.

Some studies suggest that setting objectives will improve a person's use of time by a minimum of 15 percent. This is equivalent to "finding" an extra hour a day that could be reinvested in the mission of the church. On an annual basis, each leader could gain the equivalent of 30 working days each year. Projecting this through 40 years increases the potential service of an individual by 1,240 days. This is convertible to 248 weeks or a minimum of five additional years of service to others.

How we choose to disburse our time is a personal matter. By default we can *allow* others to overload each of our 365 calendar squares with tasks tangential and extraneous to our mission in life. Or we can develop, regularly review, and work toward our priority goals and objectives. Only then will we be in a position to weigh each new time demand against these targets and increase the probability that our time is indeed invested in God's work.

4. "Can't Say No" Syndrome

Many conscientious leaders sound as if they were born with a yes in their mouth. One such leader reportedly vowed he would say no to the next person imposing on his time. Later when leaned on by a friend, he struggled for a moment and replied, "No-kay."

Problems of Always Saying Yes

Many leaders lament the fact that they never seem to have enough time. They suffer from a common problem—a fearfulness about using the word "no," the greatest time-saving tool in the English language. A can't-say-no syndrome *dis-tracks* leaders from their basic life objectives. Leaders never will have time to do everything that others want them to.

As leaders we find it tempting to say yes for some of the wrong reasons. These include

1. a desire to gain the approval and acceptance of others. It is natural for leaders to want to be liked. Yet we may forget whose approval comes first—that of other human beings or of God;

2. a fear of offending friends or acquaintances. Yet a candid statement kindly offered about our present priority commitments seldom is offensive to others;

3. a feeling of low self-esteem. It is probable that leaders saying yes to all requests may have a compelling need to be needed by others;

4. a tendency to overrate our own sense of importance. Some leaders act as if no one else could possibly do their tasks as well or as fast. So they retain numerous assignments of relatively low importance.

The effective leader allocates adequate time to identify the organization's major goals and objectives. Once these are developed and adopted, the leader will strive to devote significant time and effort to the fulfillment of the organization's major mission. A less effective leader abuses God-given time when neglecting basic objectives and allowing less significant or extraneous activities to consume scarce hours.

A point of balance can be found between always saying yes or always saying no. Leaders need to examine each time demand on its own merits. Valid questions include

1. How closely does this request for my time match our organization's basic objectives?
2. If I accept this request for _____ hours of my time, which of my primary tasks will I postpone or drop? What effect will this have on my ability to fulfill organizational objectives?
3. Am I actually avoiding an important but difficult duty by accepting a new responsibility that "justifies" neglecting my basic mission?

Those with responsible positions must eliminate activities of lesser relevance if they are to make time available for major responsibilities. A church leader, for example, may find it enjoyable to assist the city council and spend many hours on special subcommittee assignments. It is ego satisfying to be a governor's appointee on state boards. The time of pastors or priests may be imprudently spent sitting through three-hour banquets or convention programs which follow a one-minute invocation. Few individuals are ever enticed to come to church through this formal ritual. On the other hand, such invocations offer an excellent opportunity for witnessing by the ministry of the laity.

The greater the number of talents a leader possesses, the more essential is an ability to say no. Saying yes to unending requests inevitably results in leaders being spread so thin they can't fulfill the basic purposes of their calling.

The Art of Persuasive Refusals

Prudent leaders will plan in advance how to respond to those who would encroach on their limited hours. The best way to set aside time for important objectives is to refuse appeals to work on less significant, time-consuming activities. The following suggestions will be helpful:

1. If a specific time request comes from a superior, discuss the high-priority tasks for which you presently are responsible. Ask where the new project belongs in relation to others on your list. Inquire which task you might defer or drop when assuming the new responsibility.
2. To miscellaneous time requests from others, simply reply, "No, I'm sorry I can't help you now." You may choose to give a brief explanation, although you have no obligation to give reasons for your refusal. Share any helpful information such as a suggestion of someone else who may assist. There are many capable young persons or others new to an organization who are willing to serve but have never been asked due to our habit of thinking mainly of "veteran" workers.
3. Respond, "Thanks for the compliment, but I'll have to decline. The task is not compatible with my governing board's priorities set for this year."
4. If pressured by an individual, just repeat, "I'm sorry but I have made other promises that I couldn't keep were I to say yes to you."
5. Counter with, "Unfortunately I don't have the 10 (or other number) hours it would take me to do your project well."
6. Explain that "it just wouldn't be fair to our staff to take on anything more unless we get extra help or drop some of our present responsibilities."
7. Simply reply, "You've caught me at a bad time. I'm already overinvolved."
8. When you chose to say yes, indicate the duration of your involvement, such as, "I will work on the ad hoc committee for three months," or, "I will serve as secretary of the organization for one year."
9. A leader's family should be high on a priority list. Be ready

to respond, "Thursday night is one time I save for my family."

10. When approached by one of the world's most convincing petitioners, make a single reply. For example, you may respond, "I won't have the time required this winter." Then repeat that one response like a broken record regardless of the person's pressure and persuasive skills.

Feeling indispensable to everything that goes on results in some leaders concluding that only they can do many things so well or so quickly. The leader who fails to ask would-be volunteers for help makes them feel unnecessary, unwanted, and incompetent. After delegating a responsibility, the leader intervenes at the first hint of trouble errs by taking over rather than talking over. During meetings some leaders so monopolize the discussion with their presence, comments, and suggestions that the morale of other would-be participants is devastated. A feeling of being indispensable impels some leaders to assume responsibility for numerous activities that steal time from their basic calling.

A subliminal desire to be liked compels many leaders to accept an excessive number of demands on their time. While the work of their oganization may suffer, the real victims are those the unit was established to serve. How foolish then is my drive to be liked? How much am I exploiting those my organization is dedicated to serve? How much "goodwill" can the organization and I afford?

5. Procrastination, the Great Putoff _____

Why, God, am I so gifted at procrastinating some major responsibilities while granting time to minor tasks? Why do I have numerous excuses for putting off a visit to a friend whose spouse died? Another friend is depressed but I postpone that first contact. Why do I permit interruptions to usurp time from my morning devotions? Why do I delay telling loved ones how important each is to me? As H. G. Bohn said, "One of these days soon becomes none of these days."

If only I received credit for my good intentions! My spirit is willing but my actions lag far behind. I sometimes wonder if Paul didn't experience similar challenges. Was he thinking of procrastination in Romans 7:18-19 when he wrote, "Though the will to do good is there, the deed is not. The good which I want to do, I fail to do"(NEB)?

It's not enough to rationalize that my postponing is only a normal, human failing. Poor habits unchallenged grow stronger each day. For some of us, procrastination becomes a hazardous habit. Because it usually involves breaking a commitment to ourselves, continual postponement brings feelings of anxiety, guilt, and stress.

Simply stated, procrastination is the continued avoidance of starting a task and seeing it to conclusion. It is also a matter of doing easier, low-priority work instead of more difficult, higher-priority tasks. Instead of finishing next year's budget, I straighten out the mess on my desk. Rather than discipline an employee, I phone the travel bureau about reservations for next summer's vacation. I major in the minors. Research shows that delaying decisions and actions fails to improve their quality. This contradicts the favorite theory of some leaders that putting things off somehow is sure to make them better.

There are two sides to the coin of procrastination. With tongue in cheek, Les Wass, president of the Procrastinator's Club of America, claims that "procrastinators lead more relaxed lives. If you're always rushing, you get to the end of your life sooner. . . . Then they call you 'the late so and so.' We feel it's better to be called 'late' while you're still alive." Procrastination can be positive *if* we actually postpone the low-priority tasks that keep us from our most important goals and objectives.

According to Odette Pollar, a few individuals find some advantages in procrastination. Putting things off may gain attention for the one who postpones. As a result there may be a psychological advantage in procrastinating, since some persons find negative attention preferable to being ignored. Then the person who finally finishes an overdue project is in line for some positive acclaim. Unfortunately, there usually is little recognition for the person who quietly gets a job done on time.

The problem of tardiness is related to procrastination. We all have friends who are late to meetings. Their excuse is that they have no sense of time. If that were factual, wouldn't they be ahead of time as often as they are late?

Causes of Procrastination

We find many reasons for deferring action on important tasks. Two of the powerful delaying forces are dislike of an important task and the avoidance of an overwhelming responsibility.

1. I have been avoiding an unpleasant job at home for two years. Earlier I had repainted all the house exterior except for the bedroom windows on one end of the house. Why? Those windows contain 72 panes, 5-1/2 x 8-1/2 inches, in wooden frames. Each frame requires two coats of paint. It was a difficult, unpleasant chore facing me. In th interim I have completed many other tasks of lesser importance.

2. Some challenges may be so difficult they seem overpowering. For example, I plan to eat less sweets and ice cream to reduce my waistline—after Christmas season is over. I'll study the new "simplified" income tax forms—when I find more time. I'll tackle the job of cataloging all the family slides—when I figure out a simple filing system. How easy it is to defer challenging tasks.

There are a number of other reasons for procrastination that seem valid on the surface:

3. Perfectionists defer actions because of abnormally high self-expectations—such as faultlessness. Fearing failure, they delay tackling a problem to avoid disappointing themselves by falling short of their goals. They tend to confuse the reasonable objective—doing the best they can with an unreasonable goal—with doing the best that's ever been done. Fearful that others may discover an error, their decision making twists in the wind. They welcome interruptions that prevent them from facing the task. For them, "not now" easily translates to "never."

4. Many of us await flashes of inspiration for problems faced. Lacking answers, we engage in continual debate on a problem, hoping that some light will turn on, lead us in the right direction, and spare us from making a tough decision. But inspiration may visit the procrastinator once for the many times it calls on a person to be perceptive and decisive. This is not to suggest that waiting for God's timing is inaction. When others urged Jesus to go up to Jerusalem while the festival crowds were there, Jesus replied, "My time has not yet come." For the leader who sincerely waits to discern the Spirit's timing, such waiting can be action.

5. For some individuals postponing is an inability to overcome inertia. As someone has said, "It's not that I procrastinate, I just have a problem with implementation." Eventually an internal reluctance to start a project begins to feed upon itself. A type of addictive enslavement follows. This type of procrastinator sleeps on any and every decision or action regardless of its importance.

6. Parents who did more for us than advisable probably contributed to our procrastination. If they regularly completed chores that we left undone, we learned that nothing serious happens when we postpone our work. Another kind of parent may have contributed to our perfectionism with the admonition, "If it's worth doing at all, it's worth doing well."
7. Overscheduling of personal responsibilities often forces an individual to resort to procrastination. Couple this with a failure to prioritize these tasks and tackle the important work first and it becomes practically impossible to complete significant duties on time.
8. Ill health and fatigue may lead to procrastination. The will to start tough jobs requires both purpose and physical stamina.

Results of Procrastination

As we postpone starting our work, we keep busy puttering with evasive actions. We find it increasingly difficult either to initiate action or gain results. Newton's physical law of inertia reveals that tasks at rest tend to stay at rest. Psychologically, the longer we allow a job to remain at rest, the greater the effort needed to overcome inertia. Consequently, the job seems to get progressively more difficult the longer we dodge it.

Procrastination puts a strain on our relationships with associates. Years ago I worked with a supervisor who had a real block when it came to decision making. When I brought completed staff work to him with a recommended course of action, his standard response was, "Let's sit on this for a while. We may have more helpful information in a week or two." He continually stalled employee hopes for action. It was frustrating to be on a team where the leader seemed afflicted with paralysis of analysis.

The one who suffers most from this malady is the procrastinator. If we regularly place important work on "hold" we begin to feel guilty, experience stress, and reinforce a poor self-image. The unfinished responsibilities nag at us and spoil the joy we should find in accomplishments. Our delaying and indecision result in discouragement, irritation, and self-disappointment.

Procrastination is a complex problem. Unchallenged, it

drains away enormous amounts of energy, enthusiasm, and time. We can change some of our undesirable habits, however, if we are willing to exert effort in accordance with the admonition in Ecclesiastes 9:10, "Work hard at whatever you do" (TEV).

Understanding Procrastination Better

Writing this book has offered me new opportunities to experience the cunning ways of procrastination. I often think of a story about Victor Hugo. He had his servants confiscate his clothes during the hours set aside for his writing. They were not allowed to return his clothing until his daily writing time was up.

Our intentions are good when we face an important but difficult task. We tell ourselves, "This one postponement is just a temporary action." Yet by sequencing a succession of little delays we wind up not starting the task—even though we've never consciously said, "I won't do this work."

To tackle procrastination we need as many facts as possible. Honest self-observation plus a listing of the tasks we put off are essential if we would understand our problem. It is also important to give ourselves permission to be human—to make errors. A mistake simply offers us a chance to make the needed correction.

Techniques for Overcoming Procrastination

The causes of procrastination are not the same for every person. As a result, each individual is the best judge of which of the following techniques is most helpful. While changing habits is never easy, we can develop new habit patterns that will help us in the future.

1. First list all the tasks you tend to procrastinate. Then prioritize that list from the most to the least important functions. Can some be delegated? Can some be dropped? Can you trade an unwanted task for your help to another person?
2. Of the remaining important tasks, decide how much time you will spend daily on each major task. Make reasonable self-expectations. If there's one you're dreading, set aside 15 minutes and give that job all you have during that time. Overcoming inertia may even carry you some distance into the

task. Gradually increase the time allotted. Accept no outside interruptions and allow no self-interruptions during that time.

3. Develop the habit of scheduling some high priority tasks each working day. Complete tomorrow's "to-do" list today. I've often been surprised at the number of helpful ideas that come to me between the time I complete tomorrow's list and the time I start work the next morning.

4. Break a difficult task into manageable segments. Losing 25 pounds may sound impossible. An objective of first losing five pounds is more achievable. Then try for the second five pounds. Completing a small first target is important because inertia is defeated. The momentum can spur us on to continued action.

5. Utilize the fact that energy levels vary throughout the day. If you are a "morning person," schedule work on your tough, important jobs during your prime time. Schedule easier tasks when you are less attentive.

6. Set definite deadlines for the total task and for each intermediate target. Inform others of your time commitments. With larger projects, post your time line on the wall. We usually feel more obligated to meet deadlines which have been shared with others.

7. To help break inertia on a tough project, schedule a calendar appointment to tackle the problem with a paid or a volunteer co-worker. Not only are we obligated to begin at that time, but we have the help and encouragement of another.

8. Promise yourself a reward when you complete a first segment or the entire project. Be sure you give yourself the reward as that practice will encourage you to stick to your next job.

9. Complete repetitive responsibilities well in advance of due dates. We may complete lesson plans or write a weekly column one week ahead of the normal schedule. This takes no additional time overall and it reduces tensions we inflict on ourselves when pushing deadlines to their limit.

10. Recognize the torment we inflict on ourselves when we are procrastination-prone. The undone tasks harass us. We suffer from self-doubts, anxiety, and lowered self-esteem. Our tac-

kling of significant but tough tasks enhances self- respect and our service to God's people.

Conclusion

Those of us struggling with procrastination are not unlike many of our associates—or the apostle Paul. We can imagine his feelings of self-reproach as he wrote in Romans 7:15, "I do not understand my own actions. For I do not do what I want" (RSV).

Most of us would like to put procrastination out of our lives promptly and painlessly. But we can't easily transform habits that did not develop overnight. A thoughtful analysis and understanding of our reasons for postponing can alter our attitude toward the problem. Transformed attitudes become mainsprings to modified behavior. While miraculous changes are possible, many of us will experience smaller growth increments that over time will lead to significant improvements.

Few of us find any pleasure in putting things off. Actually it's a high-priced practice when we consider loss of time, loss of self-esteem, and loss of mission fulfillment. It's much more rewarding to be a doer than a stewer.

"On with it, then, and finish the job! Be as eager to finish it as you were to plan it" (2 Corinthians 8:11 TEV).

6. Planning and Prioritizing___

Records show that of 2,234 ships leaving port 2,233 arrive at their destination. As crew leader, the ship's captain has a definite goal, an explicit plan of action, and the perseverance to avoid detouring to other attractive harbors.

Planning is the highest leadership function. Leaders failing to plan find trivial work expanding to fill every unplanned minute. Continual crises drive them in haphazard directions. They lose their perspective of what's really important.

The more time that leaders devote to planning, the more success the organization experiences. Dun and Bradstreet completed a survey of factors that distinguish the best U.S. companies from typical organizations. They found that leaders in the more productive companies spent 75 percent or more of their time planning. Other studies reveal that 70 percent of us tend to plan just one day at a time.

Christian leadership is too important to be controlled by unpredictable and random events. The more pressures a leader has for his time, the more crucial it is to make weekly and daily plans that focus on long-range organizational goals.

Why Leaders Fail to Plan

There are a number of probable reasons why we as leaders overlook the important planning functions.

1. While we consider it important, planning is seldom urgent. We postpone planning because it's simpler to react to emergencies. We disregard the fact that better planning reduces the frequency of crisis.

2. Planning is often a difficult, even distasteful task.
3. Because it involves the future, planning does not offer immediate rewards nor the sense of accomplishment we get from completing small tasks.
4. Planning makes us accountable for some expected results. We no longer can postpone action. We must face the issues involved.
5. It is tempting to major in the minors. We rationalize that we will get the small tasks out of the way first, forgetting we always will face an endless stream of minutiae.
6. Planning forces us to deal with future uncertainties. To the extent that we fear making mistakes, we are induced to procrastinate.
7. Scheduling time to plan requires changing some habits and relinquishing some preferred, enjoyable tasks.
8. Planning involves skills for which many leaders have had no specific training.

Why Planning Is Important

As leaders we are responsible for making a conscious choice to schedule a portion of each day for planning. Neglecting this, trivial tasks from a multitude of persons will absorb our time.

Many leaders are like puppets whose strings are pulled by an unorganized crowd of special-interest persons. The larger an organization, the more persons seek a part of the leader's time. Leaders must establish priorities as to how they will spend time, for there won't be enough time for both long-range objectives and all the immediate, urgent demands.

It is impossible to "save time." We regularly spend every minute as soon as it arrives. But we can spend our time more wisely. We need to avoid the activity trap of simply keeping busy. Instead, we should think in terms of investing and earning greater results from the time we spend.

As someone said, "I was so busy cutting down the trees that I didn't have time to sharpen my saw." We give in to the crunch and pace of daily activities, which become so hectic that our continual motion prevents us from achieving our major objectives.

One illustration deals with an exercise in assembling small

models called "widgets." Two groups of people in different rooms received written instructions and the parts with which to assemble widgets. The leader told one group to begin the assembly task immediately. The leader instructed members in the second group not to touch the parts for 10 minutes. Which group excelled? The group forced to wait 10 minutes, during which time they read the instructions and planned their work. Members organized their task by deciding who would assume which responsibility. They assembled all their widgets while the first group was still struggling along in typical disorganization.

Though the contrasts are more easily seen in the physical realm, similar results apply in all organizational work. Leaders are active persons who often tend to move ahead quickly with a task before developing a procedural plan. The enticing trap of continual activity often sabotages our attention to basic organizational objectives.

It is seldom, if ever, possible for leaders to control all their working hours. Yet every time we start work without clear-cut objectives, we automatically react to agendas established by others. The average leader in our society spends one-third or less time on truly important tasks. The work of Christian organizations is too important to be handicapped by lack of planning.

How to Make Time for Planning

A leader must make time for planning; it will not be "found." Every leader now spends the entire allotment of 168 hours a week. *If we are to allocate time for planning, we must first reduce the hours currently spent on other functions.* As Henry Mintzberg said, "Hoping to find time for general planning is tantamount to hoping that the pressures of the job will go away." If we fail to selectively neglect some current activities, we will not be successful in allotting time for planning.

Leaders can get more done in one quiet hour than in a day filled with endless interruptions. Several descriptors can be used for time devoted to an individual's planning. These include "quiet time," a "closed period," or "hideaway time." I prefer the term "planned unavailability." A leader's availability to every passer-by raises some provoking questions. Has the leader chosen to be indispensable? Is it possible that the leader has a "need to be needed"? We should face that question squarely, particularly if we suffer from continual interruptions due to our "open-door policy."

A genuine emergency can interrupt time reserved for planning. But all emergencies are not equally important. The leader should evaluate and judge each crisis in comparison to the important objectives already established for the week.

When I was a high school principal, a student burst into my office half an hour after school one day. Excitedly, he announced that someone had nailed shut the industrial arts classroom door and the teacher could not get out to go home. I was tempted to act as if the emergency required my getting the teacher out . . . and become a hero. After comparing the urgency of the situation with my need to continue writing staff evaluation reports, I phoned the secretary to ask the custodian to let the teacher out. It is not easy for those of us addicted to handling crises to break that habit, but we must do so if we are to set aside time for planning.

Planned Availability and Planned Unavailability

It is productive if leaders establish and announce "reception hours" when they normally will be available to drop-ins. It is equally important that leaders initiate some quiet time for planned unavailability—a time of accepting no phone calls, visitors, or other interruptions—a time that will encourage attention to the important task of planning.

A mutual insurance company in Michigan has a quiet or closed period for their employees daily from 8 to 9 a.m. Frequent callers know to avoid phoning at this time. The company employees soon discovered that their whole day was positively influenced—that as the first hour went, so went their day. Some claimed they accomplished almost half a day's work in the uniterrupted morning hour.

With no quiet hour it takes a firm resolve for persons to drop their socializing and start on their most important task the first thing each morning. First clearing up some trivial items prevents the leader from getting to the important tasks. A steadfast refusal to be involved in any minutiae for the first hour will bring exemplary results.

A national forest ranger district in Nevada established quiet hours from 10 a.m. till noon each day with excellent results. The city hall in Carnation, Washington, is closed for planning purposes every Wednesday from 8:30 a.m. till noon. In another town the church staff of four has three members unavailable each morning till 11:30. Most banks are closed to customer service for two hours each morning. Don't discard the suggestion of a quiet time for planning with a quick evaluation that "it won't work here."

A leader can set aside time for planning by placing his own name on his calendar for an hour each day. The secretary can cooperate by informing callers that the calendar is filled at that hour.

Some leaders use two other novel approaches to provide an opportunity for planning. The first is to locate a "hideaway," a different area in the vicinity (library, conference room, storage area, etc.), and use it as a retreat for planning purposes. Another approach is to spend the first working hour of each day at home without the usual office interruptions.

The value of an early hour, quiet hour, or similar time of unavailability lies in the fact that concentrated time is vastly more productive than scattered time. During times of concentration a leader can develop the momentum necessary to move a project along. Without an uninterrupted block of time to concentrate efforts on long-range tasks, planning becomes impossible and an organization's basic objectives are abandoned by default. Given the importance of their work, Christian leaders cannot defend the practice of small-task hopping.

Advantages of Planning

1. Someone has said, events that are scheduled are more likely to happen.
2. Some studies suggest that leaders can save three hours for every hour invested in planning . . . and the results are better.
3. Daily schedules should leave several hours for unpredictable but certain-to-occur interruptions. Without such built-in flexibility the day's schedule is doomed to fail.

4. Annual goals and objectives established by a governing body help to safeguard leaders from a vast array of personal priorities dropped on them by a large number of unorganized individuals.
5. A consensus on organizational goals can be achieved.
6. Leaders become objective oriented. They become more proactive rather than reacting to emergencies.
7. A high correlation exists between an effective leader and the amount of time spent on the important organizational objectives.

The Group Planning Process—Major Steps

A more structured format is required for group planning sessions. The following steps are my adaptation of some guidelines originally developed for the Xerox Corporation.

1. Allot ample time for the planning process, a minimum of 75 to 90 minutes.
2. Invite a moderate number (eight or less) of knowledgeable and competent persons to a conference area free of distractions.
3. Begin with the question, "What seems to be the problem?" Through discussion of relevant factors, reach agreement on the real problem.
4. Share any known or anticipated restrictions to the solution, such as limits in funding, staffing, or time for the project.
5. Ask participants, "What do you think we should do?" As group leader, curb the temptation to unfurl your answer before listening to the contributions of all others. Thereafter, if your solution is still pertinent, place it on the table with the others for consideration.
6. Evalute each alternative solution by writing down its advantages and disadvantages.
7. Seek consensus on what the group sees as the best overall approach.
8. Develop a specific action plan. Decide which participant will be responsible for each action item identified. Designate a completion date for each task.

9. Restate all the tasks, persons responsible, and due dates. Close the session.

If the action plan proposed will extend over a period of time (several months to years), a simple time line will help all involved meet their responsibilities. This procedure displays each task above the time line, person(s) responsible for a task immediately below the line, and the completion date above each task near the top of the page. Participants are reminded of their responsibilities and of due dates if the time line is posted in the leader's office and a copy given to each person involved.

Planning Your Next Week—Major Steps

Planning for the next week starts at a Friday afternoon meeting with the leader's secretary and any assistant(s). The agenda should include

1. examining the past week's successes and failures;
2. identifying major objectives for the next week;
3. limiting the number of objectives to a manageable few (we tend to overestimate our ability and underestimate the time needed for completion);
4. evaluating the objectives selected for consistency with organizational goals;
5. asking *what, where, how, when,* and *who* for each objective: know specifically *what* the objective is, *where* it fits on the priority list, *how* many hours estimated for completion by *when,* the completion deadline, and *who* is responsible for its completion;
6. listing the activities needed to complete each objective. This is done by the individual responsible for the action. It reduces procrastination by breaking projects into smaller components for easier disposition;
7. distributing and reviewing copies of the weekly plan with all leadership team members on Monday morning.

Realize that human plans are not etched in stone. Consider them helpful guides for future action until you adjust them to conform to new or more accurate facts not previously available.

Planning Your Daily Schedule—Major Steps

Scheduling activities for each day is one of the best ways to avoid wasting time. Without daily planning, leaders run the risk of being crisis controlled.

Complete planning of the next day's activities before leaving the office the previous afternoon. This gives your subconcious 15 hours to work on tomorrow's challenges. The tasks listed should further one of the objectives in the weekly plan. Your daily schedule should

1. list the day's prioritized activities;
2. estimate the time required for completion of each activity;
3. list all meetings, appointments, and prioritized tasks on a daily schedule sheet broken into 15-minute intervals;
4. bunch related functions on the schedule (returning phone calls, reading mail, aswering mail, etc.);
5. schedule your thinking on "concentration activities" at your best time of the day set aside for your planned unavailability;
6. build in "slack time" (a quarter to a third of your day) for unplanned demands on your time (a day completely scheduled will seldom be successful);
7. compare each emergency with the important tasks already on your calendar before letting anything disrupt your daily plans.

Realize that if you can control even two hours a day (time at your personal discretion), you are doing well in time management. Second, meet with your secretary as early as possible every day. Keep her fully informed of your day's planned activities plus any and all changes in your priorities. Co-workers resent appearing incompetent or ignorant. When uninformed, they are ill equipped to serve as cooperative team members.

Summary

Regular planning on a weekly and daily basis will not come easily to those with limited planning experience. Years of "winging it" and responding to crises will leave ingrained habits troublesome to overcome. The first reaction of many persons wishing to be successful leaders is, "But I can't find time to plan!"

On the other hand, leaders should refrain from browbeating themselves for not being perfect planners and performers. Few of us qualify as experts. After years of study and after offering numerous seminars on this topic, I still know more about time management than I practice. Consistent attention, however, to planning activities that move us in the direction of God's purposes is too crucial a goal to be left to happenstance.

Those with leadership responsibilities should persevere in daily efforts to perfect their planning skills. Evaluating each previous day's accomplishments will improve planning for the next day. Slowly, but surely, our planning skills will become more effective. We'll be less at the mercy of countless interruptions regardless of their importance or unimportance. Best of all, we'll find a deeper joy and contentment as well as a sense of greater personal responsibility for our time invested as servants of the Servant.

7. Effective Verbal Communication

There is nothing as easy as talking,
and nothing as difficult as communicating.
(Unknown)

Introduction

While communication of the "Word" is the basic mission of the church, mis-communication with words may be a leader's greatest timewaster. This challenge is not unique to religious organizations. A study of attempts to achieve excellence in 198 companies located in the United States, Great Britain, and Japan found that their number one barrier was poor communication.

Many leaders spend 85 percent of their workday communicating. Further analysis reveals that over 40 percent of that time is lost in irrelevant talk, unnecessary details, useless digressions, and conversational "fat."

Effective communication is the hallmark of competent leadership. Confusion results, however, when we assume that
1. if we have learned to read, we possess listening skills;
2. if we present either a written or oral message, we have communicated;
3. if we are nonverbal, we don't communicate.

This chapter deals with the importance of listening, the importance of focusing on the central theme in a message, the value of two-way communication, the helpful skill of paraphrasing, and suggestions for leaders seeking to increase meaningful communication.

Are You Listening?

They have ears, but do not hear.
(Psalm 115:6)

Listening is a lost art for many individuals. Leaders are no exception. As human beings we tend to be self-centered. We find it difficult to listen because that requires us to focus our attention on the interest of others. Typically we are so intent on what we wish to say that we fail to attend to what others say.

I reviewed the entries on "speaking" and "listening" in Rhoda Tripp's book, *The International Thesaurus of Quotations*. It contained 61 quotations on speaking and only 5 on listening. In our society do we consider speaking 12 times as important as listening?

Sperry Corporation has sponsored valuable studies on listening. They suggest that the present emphasis in communication skills in our schools is the opposite of what is needed. Typically schools stress reading, writing, speaking, and listening in that order. The report suggests reversing the priority order since listening skills are so critically important.

The Sperry listening study included a questionnaire titled, "How Well Do You Listen?" It asked individuals to rate themselves as listeners. Only 15 percent rated themselves superior, excellent, or above average, while 85 percent considered themselves average, below average, poor, or terrible. Another part of the questionnaire asked participants to grade themselves as listeners on a scale of 0 to 100. The average self-rating was 55 percent. A second query asked these persons how they thought others would rate them as listeners. Participants estimated their boss and best friends would rate them higher than 55 percent; work colleagues or subordinates would rate them at the 55-percent level; while their spouse would rate them below 55 percent, with the score decreasing as the total years of marriage increased.

A Tuned-Out Generation

Most of us find it difficult to change our listening traits. We spend more time perfecting nonlistening or tuning-out skills than we do attempting to improve our listening habits. We have expanded our tuning-out practices from background music, radio, and television programs to the tuning out of teachers, ministers, co-workers, and family members. We exemplify a "tuned-out" generation.

In talking to his associates, the New Testament writer James says, "Of that you may be certain, my friends. . . . each of you must be quick to listen, slow to speak, and slow to be angry" (James 1:19 NEB). Another person has said that an eternal talker neither listens nor learns.

With reasonable effort, leaders can modify their turned-off listening habits. Some basic helps for improved listening include
1. focusing on the person speaking;
2. resisting distractions;
3. concentrating on the content or the ideas presented;
4. disregarding the style of delivery;
5. keeping an open mind;
6. being alert to the emotional content of the words heard;
7. anticipating what may be said next.
8. using feedback to verify the accuracy of your understanding.

Since feedback is such a strategic tool in fruitful communication, special attention will be given this skill.

Paraphrasing—Worth Its Weight in Gold

> *I know you believe you understand*
> *what you think I said, but I am*
> *not sure you realize that what*
> *you heard is not what I meant.*
> *(Unknown)*

Most of us assume that we understand what the other person intended to convey. Genuine understanding, however, rarely occurs. Paraphrasing is an effective skill in which I state in my own words what your remark conveys to me. Then you can determine whether your message was perceived as intended. Paraphrasing is a simple but often neglected conversational tool which can increase communication accuracy.

A simple example of feedback follows.

Teacher A claims, "This Bible history book is just no good!"

Teacher B responds with her interpretation of the sender's message. "You mean that the facts are inaccurate or that it is poorly written?"

Teacher A, speaking to the specific misunderstandings, "Oh, no. But the binding is poorly done and the pages begin to fall out after the book has been used a short time."

As speakers we know the message we intend to convey. Yet the listener usually assumes the message received is that which the sender intended. Failure to verify the actual message allows for distortion, misinterpretation, and dissension.

I served as consultant to a church council where two subgroups were in complete disagreement on an issue. I asked a person in group A to paraphrase the thinking of the group B members. The attempt was made. Group B members, however, responded with exasperation. They spurted out, "You're not listening. That's not what we're saying!" Then I asked group B members to paraphrase the thinking of those in group A. The results were similar. It's amazing how intelligent adults can be so intent on getting their own ideas across that they ignore concentrating on what others wish to share with them.

In my Time Management seminars I use an exercise where participant A looks at a picture on the screen while participants B, C, D, E, and F are outside the room. One of them at a time comes back into the room. First A tells B what she has seen projected on the screen; next C reenters the room and B tells C what he has heard. This continues till F returns, listens to E's account, and then gives his own report. As you can imagine, the message has become seriously distorted. More interesting is the fact that only about five percent of all participants ask any questions or stop to check their understanding of the message they heard, with a paraphrase. Their actions suggest that they believe, "What I understand is more important to me than what you actually meant."

The strategic value of paraphrasing is that it surfaces specific points of misunderstanding for immediate clarification. Without such communication correction, leaders may find their paid or volunteer co-workers diligently working—but at the wrong tasks.

In my communicating efforts I find the following two feedback techniques helpful. After listening to what you say, I comment, "I don't always listen too carefully. I want to understand what you are saying. Is this correct?" Then I restate in my own words what I think you said. On the other hand, when sharing information with you I turn the technique around. I request that you paraphrase my thoughts with this comment: "I don't always explain my thinking too clearly. Would you tell me in your own words what you think I meant?" If a communication error exists, I can correct the actual misunderstanding.

Paraphrasing not only increases the accuracy of information shared by the leader, but it demonstrates interest in and respect for the other person's thinking. It conveys feeling of mutual concern and helps to defuse emotional problems. Paraphrasing *is* worth its weight in gold.

Pitfalls of One-Way Communication

One Leader's Communication Philosophy
1. The leader is always right.
2. If the leader is wrong, see rule No.1.

Some leaders rely heavily on one-way communication. Apparently they assume that dynamic leaders don't need to listen to co-workers or that listening is not worth the time invested.

It is said that Winston Churchill had a unique interpretation of the word "conversation"—he was always up to bat, and it was the job of all others to field.

This is not a foreign perspective for some leaders. A representative of a bridge construction company asked if I would speak at their semiannual conference. Before accepting I asked about their plans for that day. The entire program was downward communication. First there was a presentation about a bridge failure in southeast Asia and next a talk by the company comptroller. After lunch I would discuss effective time management practices. Following a coffee break the president would talk about the company's plans—and the session would be dismissed. Employees from the western states were to be fielders the entire day for a few preselected batters. In my opinion employee reaction would be, "Apparently I have nothing worth management's time to contribute in spite of my extensive field experience."

I declined the company's invitation with a suggestion that they substitute a session for two-way communication during my scheduled time. "But we've always done it the other way," was their first reaction. Later I checked and found they had followed my suggestion with mixed results. At first the session was rather stormy—the lid had been on the kettle too long. The leaders admitted, however, that the two-way communication session became the most productive portion of the entire day.

It is easy to forget that our associates often return what we model for them. If we habitually use one-way communication, we develop hostile rather than listening colleagues. John Wooden, legendary UCLA basketball coach, philosophized, "Why don't we realize that others are more certain to listen to us if we first listen to them?"

There are some classic exercises contrasting one-way and two-way communication. One involves two small groups whose leaders, looking at a configuration of rectangles, instruct their workers to draw a duplicate of that design on their paper. Since leader and workers sit back to back, neither can see the work of others. Group A can't talk to or ask any questions of their leader. So leader A bats and the workers try to make sense out of whatever comes their way. At times their frustration level becomes so intense I have seen a worker stand up, crumple his worksheet, throw it on the floor and stalk out of the room. Group B's results using two-way communication are clearly superior. Here the workers are allowed to question their leader and any of her instructions. In this situation the workers gain confidence as they progress, develop a team feeling, sense a cooperative relationship with their leader, and exhibit much higher morale.

At first the task seems more difficult for leader B, who communicates with co-workers. Her directions are questioned. She hears suggestions that may differ from the original plans. In the long run, however, the leader gains a confidence the one-way leader never experiences. Her workers' reactions assure leader B the workers have mastered the project, they know they have mastered the project, and they experience renewed confidence and pride.

"Conversational Fat" Clogs Communication

*A flow of words is not always
a flow of wisdom.*
(Rosalind Fergusson)

Putting conversations and memos on a diet will save significant time in communicating.

Charles Ford, consultant in organizational behavior, analyzed 18 leaders in a number of companies to determine how they spent their conversational time. He reported they spent five and one-half hours a day in communication. More surprising, the study reported that two hours a day were wasted on what he termed "conversational fat." These irrelevant discussions, digressions, excess details, and socialization become more serious when converted to the equivalent of 13 weeks each year lost through conversational fat.

Earlier a communication exercise was described where one participant looked at a picture which later was described to five other persons. A second learning from that exercise is pertinent here. The picture had a central theme—two men standing in the middle of a bus or subway having a serious confrontation. Those reporting what they saw, however, allotted less time to the central theme than they did to many irrelevant details such as a flower in one woman's hat, a red cap worn by a baby, a man's yellow socks, and one woman's gold collar. Many of us are similarly tempted to overcommunicate trivia and underemphasize the central theme of what we wish to communicate.

Prior to initiating any communication, leaders should ask,
1. what is the purpose of this communication?
2. what information do I wish to convey?
3. what information should I seek?
4. what, if any, followup is needed?

To get to the heart of another person's comments, a leader may say, "I know a lot of hard work has gone into your project, but please tell me its status right now." To avoid wasting time on irrelevant topics with drop-ins a leader may state, "I'd like to talk with you, but I have some other obligations now. Can we discuss it later today or tomorrow?" Often such a topic never surfaces again.

Calvin Collidge may have been thinking of conversational fat when he said, "I have never been hurt by anything I didn't say."

Keeping Co-workers Informed

Don't ask me, I just work here!

Co-workers resent being ignorant about their organization and its activities. In 1946 the Labor Relations Institute of New York asked many employees to rank order 10 working conditions. They evaluated "Feeling of being in on things" as second most important of the 10 items. Next leaders were asked to prioritize the same 10 items as they thought *workers* would rank order them. Leaders believed workers would rank "Feeling of being in on things" ninth. The study was repeated in 1979. Employees ranked the item third in importance. Leaders thought employees would rank it 10th, or least important of the 10 working conditions.

Whenever we as leaders fail to provide accurate and thorough information, we foster misunderstandings and rumors. Prudent leaders will keep co-workers fully informed about any changes in plans or shifts in priorities.

Luke writes about Jesus telling His parable of the sower. Jesus admonished the crowd of followers, "Listen, then, if you have ears!" Later He responded to questions from His disciples. He explained to them, "This is what the parable means" (Luke 8:8, 11 TEV). He did not want His followers to be uninformed concerning His teachings.

Many leaders assume they are communicating when they talk to others. But communication is not simply the creating of sound—it is the perceiving of sound. The one who speaks is an emitter. Because the listener can tune out the message, the listener is in control of the communication process. Effective leaders realize that it is possible to communicate *only* in language that is meaningful to and understood by the recipient.

As leaders we "lose" our listeners whenever we try to impress rather than express. I have known capable individuals who would never use a 10-cent word if they could substitute several five-dollar words. They seemed unconcerned about whether or not their emission level was within or outside the listeners' range of understanding. These "leaders" suffer a silent hostility and alienation from resentful "followers."

Guidelines for More Meaningful Communication

1. Remember that communication is the reception, not the creation, of sound; therefore, communication must be in the receiver's language.
2. Determine in advance the central theme of any message you wish to communicate. Avoid all distracting details.
3. Move to your central theme in as few words as possible.
4. Use words everyone easily understands.
5. Plan each communication effort. Review your plan and ask, "Is there any way these thoughts can be misunderstood?"
6. Invite questions typical of two-way communication even though it feels "safer" to hide behind one-way communication.
7. Check your understanding of what you hear with paraphrasing. Check a co-worker's understanding of what you say by asking that person to paraphrase your statements.
8. Realize that hearing is basically an unconscious act, while listining is a difficult, intellectual activity that requires your devoted attention.
9. Direct your communications to the right persons.
10. Ask paid or volunteer workers
    a. what they wish to know about the organization;
    b. what you do that gets in their way;
    c. what pending problems they see for the organization;
    d. what existing opportunities they believe the organization is failing to utilize.

Summary

The greatest problem with communication
is the illusion that it has been achieved.
(George Bernard Shaw)

Faulty communication is a basic cause of wasted time. As one leader said, "If I make an assignment but there is some misunderstanding, all the time spent on the task can be lost, plus the time required to give correct instructions so it can be done all over again." Even small verbal misconceptions continually steal time from an organization's primary mission. In addition the personal costs of careless communication include embarrassment, antagonism, and stress.

Leaders are penny-wise and pound-foolish if they attempt to cut corners when communicating with associates. Initially they may save a few minutes by giving hurried instructions, but the long-term loss is often an expensive waste of time. Keeping others fully informed is one evidence of the leader's care and consideration for associates. Morale is notably higher when there are few if any surprises—when the verbal interchange with leaders is frequent and two-way. Simple, straightforward communication plus attentive listening and an opportunity to seek clarification are consistent with Jesus' teaching, "In everything, do to others what you would have them do to you " (Matthew 7:12 NIV).

8. Nonverbal Communication

I'll never forget the nonverbal message of a man I saw near Dacca, Bangladesh. Though he had no legs, he was traveling down the roadside. He had no wheelchair. He didn't even have a platform with wheels on which to ride. He propelled himself by rolling on the ground—from his back to his side, to his stomach, to his other side, to his back, to his side, to his stomach, and so on. Amazed, I queried my friend about him. He explained that every Friday this man goes to his mosque to give thanks and to praise God. What powerful nonverbal communication! If we "listen," his actions overwhelm many of our eloquent declarations of dedication and commitment. They remind me of the saying, "Many people will not read a Bible, but they will read a Christian."

While many of us are not very alert to nonverbal communication, it deserves more attention than we realize. In a normal day the typical leader spends 85 percent of his or her day communicating with others. The physical setting and the body language are vital parts of this communication. These not only carry a message—in some circumstances they give the dominant message.

Effective leaders listen for the silent and subtle messages evidenced by gestures, movement, posture, eyes, tone of voice, or touch. They also try to be aware of their own nonverbal communication, much of which is unintentional. These subtle messages frequently are more accurate than oral statements. Though we try to censor silent messages, they leak out and can confuse the "listener" concerning our real intent.

Verbal and Nonverbal Love

As I write this chapter our grandchild, Emily, is one week old. How do grandparents express their love for a baby? Words are of no help. We make nonsense sounds. We hold, hug, rock, and hum—and all is nonverbal.

I visited a hospitalized friend who was too ill to speak. I held her hand for a while, giving a little squeeze now and then, hoping to feel a squeeze in response. Another time I met the grieving mother at the funeral of her 25-year-old daughter. Try as I would, I found no ready words that seemed adequate for the situation. Giving her a comforting hug, however, helped me communicate my sorrow and say that I was present because I cared.

Holden Village is between the eastern slope of the Cascade Mountains and Lake Chelan in Washington. A former mining town, it now serves as a Lutheran retreat center for adults. Hikers occasionally traverse the Cascades from the Seattle side over Cloudy Pass and through Holden Village on their way to Lake Chelan. One hot summer day some villagers did more than verbalize their "Welcome" to weary hikers coming down from the pass. They invited them to sit on a low rock wall and washed their feet. The act of love was completely nonverbal but eloquently meaningful for all participants.

The power of nonverbal acts to express love should never amaze us. Our Christian faith rests primarily on Christ's self-sacrificial death—the most significant of all nonverbal acts of love.

Physical Details Also Communicate

Some leaders seem unaware of ideas communicated through the relationship of individuals and physical space. For example, tall buildings favor hierarchical relationships. Top management usually is located on the highest floor of a building.

The executive offices of the White House also are an interesting place to study nonverbal communication. Leader "A," for example, is getting new carpet, drapes, and wallpaper in his office. The message is loud and clear—this person is on his way up. Associate "B" is asked to relinquish his present office for a smaller one at the end of the corridor and near the incinerator. Again, there is little question about the silent message being communicated.

The appearance of a church building and the maintenance level of its grounds speak volumes to outsiders. An unmowed lawn, untrimmed shrubs, and abundant weeds suggest a general disinterest in physical details, an attitude of carelessness.

Some leaders who seem less secure tend to stake out an invisible boundary around their desks. It represents "safe territory" and helps maintain that person's authority role. To counteract such psychological barriers a leader should not seat a visitor on the opposite side of a desk which can appear like a "fortress." Place the visitor's chair at the side of your desk so no barrier separates you from those with whom you talk.

Imagine that your shoes wear paths wherever you walk. If you were able to look down on your community from above, your trails would reveal not only those persons you befriend but also those you avoid. The "neglected" individuals undoubtedly are aware of your nonverbal messages. Are these statements ones that you wish to send?

Messages in Facial Expressions

If there is emotional impact in a message, only 7 percent of it comes through your words; 38 percent of it comes through your tone of voice and 55 percent through your facial expression. When communicating by phone we're all handicapped by an inability to sense any emotion through unseen facial expressions.

The most powerful facial message I have read was on a mother in the Asian subcontinent. She was begging for money to buy food for her baby. I can still see the concentration in her pleading eyes as she walked beside me and moved her hand from her open mouth to the tiny baby in her arms. She could not speak English, but how effectively she communicated!

Without saying one word, a teacher can indicate she thinks a student is smart, dumb, pretty, ugly, or unimportant. Through silence, she can reveal her dislike for papers written in pencil or her preference for boy athletes in class. These situations are consistent with another study reporting that the face appears to be the most skilled of all nonverbal communicators. Its findings suggest that facial communication is rated at least three times as effective as vocal communication.

Ignorance of Our Own Nonverbals

While our own silent communication is usually honest and difficult to disguise from others, it often is unkown to us. The recommendation letters for a new teacher I once hired were excellent except for two minor comments. The teacher asked that I react to his application file. Without revealing the sources, I shared that one person reported that occasionally he appeared aloof while another said that at times he appeared distant. The new teacher responded with mixed feelings. He was unhappy that former leaders had written about these behaviors without ever sharing their evaluations with him. He was glad to learn of these reactions, saying, "I can and will do something about this problem, now that I know of it."

I believe we have a responsibility to mirror some of the unknown nonverbal traits of our associates—never in a judgmental way but simply by reporting, "Here's the way a nonverbal action of yours speaks to me."

For example, one leader may continually stress how urgent a specific mission of the church is. Yet if he spends his time largely on other tasks, associates will believe what he does instead of what he professes. In meetings we broadcast nonverbal messages when we look at one or two individuals most of the time. Others soon feel worth less. A similar situation exists if a leader is available to and spends time with a relatively limited number of individuals in the organization.

We are aware of the statement, "It's not what you say, it's the way that you say it." Some claim that 90 percent of the friction in daily life is caused by our attitude rather than the words we use. Leaders also are well advised to remember that silence can be evidence of a superb command of the English language.

Verbal and Nonverbal Contradictions

Whenever what individuals say is incompatible with what they do, observers normally will believe the nonverbal messages. This is a special challenge to those our society expects to give exemplary leadership in areas such as education and the church. Someone has said, "If the map and the terrain disagree, trust the terrain."

Reducing budgets in schools or churches highlights the challenge of being consistent with what we preach. Weighing budget items, one might be tempted to think, "The newly developed curriculum materials for improving reading skills are much needed—but we can't ruin our athletic programs," or, "We do need a part-time staff member to work with our youth next summer, but that same amount of money would complete our new-piano fund." Would a careful review of congregational budgets show a high correlation between what we verbalize as our primary mission and our allocation of financial resources? If eternal vigilance is ever needed, a searching examination of compatibility between stated organizational goals and actual expenditure categories is the place to start.

Recently my wife and I visited many churches and cathedrals in Europe. On the narthex wall of a church in Sweden was a massive granite plaque. In large letters at the top were engraved the words, "Soli Deo Gloria"—"Solely to the Glory of God." Inscribed on the lower part of the plaque in equally large letters we read: "Given by Nils Anderson and Sven Hasselquist" (names have been changed). I am confused by the memorials and monuments in many cathedrals and churches. It seems they praise mortal man while professing to be for the glory of God. I wonder sometimes where we would find Jesus sharing His message today—inside or outside some of these monumental structures memorializing individuals with memorial plaques, stained-glass windows, burial crypts, ornate baptismal fonts.

How often do our actions contradict our verbal goal of being a servant of the Servant? How large is the gap between our preaching and our acting? Are we attracted more by the prestige of being a leader than by the less-significant task of being a servant? How much consistency will others sense between our spoken declarations and our silent, revealing actions?

I was in old Jerusalem during the Greek Orthodox Holy Week. Daily through the narrow streets there were long, formal processions of church dignitaries. If we were completely honest,

I think many of us would have enjoyed the honor accorded the black-robed archbishop as his procession moved slowly through the narrow streets. Marching in front were aides rhythmically stamping long brass rods on the stone pavement to clear visitors and shoppers out of their way. I pondered the nonverbal message of pomp and privilege. Then I reflected on Jesus' words, "Whosoever will be chief among you, let him be your servant; even as the Son of Man came not to be ministered unto but to minister" (Matthew 20:27-28 KJV).

Parents, church leaders, and teachers all face a continual dilemma in working to reconcile their verbal and nonverbal communication. Children and youth probably have never been satisfied with the edict, "Do as I say and not as I do." As adults, we'll never be perfect examples for children—but we can direct them to their model in the Master Servant. And the closer we walk with Him, minute by minute, the more those we lead will contemplate Him rather than us. Then we may be surprised at how well the next generation turns out in spite of all the poor adult examples from which to learn. We'll worry less about Paul Armstrong's verse

> I never cease to wonder,
> In this age of space and speed,
> The distance still remains the same
> Between the word and deed.
> *(The Flip Side of Paul Armstrong*
> [Eugene, OR: Lane Community College Press,1971])
> Reprinted by permission of the author.

Today's conscientious leaders need to increase their awareness of nonverbal communication, carefully "listening" to what their associates' silent messages reveal. In addition, as leaders we should work to identify and attend to what our own nonverbal messages are communicating to others. This is difficult. I hear my spoken words and can monitor what I have said. I get no similar feedback from my nonverbal communication.

Our attitudes and actions can override our words. Because of this I often feel we have an obligation within the family of God to help each other by "holding up a mirror" and in love objectively dispelling the ignorance of a friend regarding his or her nonverbal communication. Our description should stop with a simple summary of what we see. No judgment or evaluative interpretation should be added to our unadorned comments.

The effective leader speaks with integrity. He or she manifests unity between and within all avenues of communication. This represents a genuine unity to recipients of the message. As Paul wrote to Timothy, "Make yourself an example to believers in speech and behaviour" (1 Timothy 4:12 NEB).

9. Written Communication

I've been a paper pamperer much of my life. I was over-impressed in my youth by a paper company motto which read, "Put it in writing. Paper remembers while people forget." In any event, my handling of written communication for many years was characterized by

1. a magnified sense of self-importance. How else could I justify a personal scrutiny of all the mail anyone wished to send my way?
2. an overactive curiosity. For what other reason would I drop ongoing work regardless of its priority to check the incoming mail whenever it hit my desk?
3. stacking and restacking of papers and periodicals. These included articles that "I will read when I have more time," in spite of the fact that I rarely found that free time.
4. insufficient confidence in a capable secretary. What other excuse could I give for not asking her to draft some letters for my signature?
5. problem procrastination. As long as a tough question was resting somewhere in my high-priority pile, I could live with my conscience. How often, however, had I picked up that problem letter, looked at it, and decided that it was not a good job for today?

Fortunately, I later learned there were better ways to deal with written communications.

A flood of paper harasses most people. Many leaders, however, fail to plan any effective flood control measure. Hence, we see desk tops covered with paper—some stratified in neat archeological mounds, others in a helter-skelter manner.

A survey by Dartnell Institute revealed that 3,000 leaders admitted they spent from two to three hours a day reading and answering mail. If we spend half that much time with our incoming mail, that is the equivalent of more than one month a year.

Incoming Mail

Time-consuming, expensive curiosity tempts many leaders to open their own mail. This is a senseless waste of time if there is anyone available to help.

1. Ask the office worker (paid or volunteer) to open and sort all incoming mail.
2. Realize that on the average only 13 percent of the mail received is of any immediate use. Specify clearly which junk mail your assistant should toss away.
3. Request that she highlight important parts of your incoming correspondence and attach any pertinent background information from the files.
4. Don't have the mail brought in at the time it is delivered. Set a time each day (after lunch?) for looking at the mail so it won't interrupt you while working on some high-priority task.
5. Feel comfortable with the fact that a capable secretary can draft replies to many of the letters you recieve.
6. Request that an assistant sort your mail into folders marked "A" for action, "B" for information, and "C" for referral to others.

Letter and Memo Writing

Leaders can trim correspondence fat by using short-form, memo-style letters. The traditional, full-page letter with long paragraphs is the dinosaur of communication.

7. Adopt the memo style for most of your correspondence. Use "To," "From," and "Subject" headings near the top of the page. Then jump into the meat of the matter with short, numbered paragraphs.
8. Keep your writing brief and to the point. Avoid big words designed to impress. Employ simple words in short sentences.

9. Use the word "you" in a conversational tone in the opening sentence. If I get a memo saying, "You asked about this," I'm more inclined to read it.
10. Write a brief handwritten reply on the original of some letters you receive. Add a sticker imprinted with, "TO SERVE YOU PROMPTLY your letter is being returned with our comments." (A rubber stamp can be used with this same message.) Ask the secretary to prepare a Xerox copy for your office and return the original to the sender. You have responded in several minutes and have saved both time and dollars. The total cost of preparing a typical business letter today varies from 6 to 10 dollars.

Dictating Equipment

Small, portable dictating devices are relatively inexpensive and save significant time. Too many leaders still write letters in longhand for later typing. We write at only 20 to 30 words per minute. Dictating speed for shorthand transcription is limited to the secretary's shorthand rate. The only limit to a machine dictation rate is the clarity of information taped for the secretary— possibly 130 to 150 words per minute. In addition, a U.S. Navy survey found that secrtetaries transcribe from a machine 33 percent faster than from either longhand or shorthand.

11. The leader gains considerable flexibility with a dictating machine. He can dictate at home, en route to meetings, at any time he has a free moment and whenever agreements and arrangements are fresh in mind. The secretary also enjoys the flexibility of transcribing at her own convenience.
12. Use two different dictation tapes—an "A" tape for priority items and a "B" tape for regular items. This helps the secretary get the important items out first.
13. Dictate in a quiet location with no background noise. State in advance the number of copies needed. Repeat vital figures and spell out unfamiliar names or terms.
14. Record a few key ideas to guide your secretary if you wish her to prepare letters for your signature.

A number of miscellaneous suggestions will help leaders become more time effective with written communication:

15. Try to handle most pieces of paper only once. We often find innumerable reasons to procrastinate more difficult items. Two approaches may help you with this problem. Every time you pick up a paper and fail to dispose of it, put an "X" on the bottom. Your habit of postponing soon becomes evident. Better yet, each time you fail to tackle the problem while handling the paper, tear off a piece and throw it away!

16. Encourage prompt replies to your inquiries by writing concise questions followed by checkoff boxes for the respondent's answer. The formulation of these questions clarifies thinking and decreases any chance for misunderstanding. It also encourgages an immediate response.

17. Install a phone-answering machine in the office. Leaders can phone when the office is closed and dictate short memos to the secretary.

18. Consider the development of several standard reply letters which the secretary can use whenever appropriate.

19. Recognize that fat files are as time costly as fat correspondence. Before selecting any paper for perpetual internment, be certain it is sufficiently important. About 90 percent of what is filed is never referred to again. Inscribe a "toss away" date on all letters given a resting place in your files.

20. Reduce file volume by using the back of the letter received for the carbon copy of your reply. This not only saves file space but it guarantees that your reply carbon will not get separated from the initiating correspondence.

21. Carry a supply of blank postcards wherever you go. Instead of writing notes to yourself about messages you want to share later, address and mail a card to the target person. Sooner than you anticipate, someone is on the phone or writing with the desired information.

   Indulging in paper piling, sorting and resorting, is a plague on the work of many leaders. Fortunately, change is possible. Attention to the recommendations in this chapter will result in leaders becoming more time-effective—alloting less time to paper and more time to people.

10. Meetings Are Too Long

Introduction

Meetings are as much a part of the American scene as baseball and apple pie. There are convincing reasons for well-outlined, productive meetings focused on planning, policy development, or the resolution of significant issues. But how do we justify unplanned, wearisome, and fruitless meetings?

One study revealed that 75 percent of the members in 200 groups insist half their time in meetings is wasted. I have asked hundreds of management seminar participants for their reaction to the statement. Normally they agree. Others claim that more than half their meeting time is valueless.

Leaders easily overlook the fact that meetings are expensive. A national PTA vice-president claims there are 11,000,000 meetings a day in the United States. I estimate the average meeting lasts two hours, that each meeting averages 10 participants, and that each person's average pay is $10 an hour. Projecting these estimates, I total a national meeting cost of $2,200,000,000 a day—plus meals, transportation, and lodging. Leaders have a responsibility to be faithful stewards of time and dollars invested in meetings.

Why the American Mania for Meetings?

A yearlong study of 300 business leaders showed that 46

percent of their time was spent in meetings. Do leaders in Christian organizations also invest almost half their time in meetings? If so, why?

1. Tradition. As one staff member grumbled, "Every Wednesday morning there's a meeting at nine o'clock—whether we need it or not. It's always been that way. The only accomplishment is that there will be another meeting next week."

2. There is an automatic assumption of legitimacy about meeting invitations. We tend to respond as if we had received a divine calling.

3. Less secure leaders tend to be afflicted with decision disability. Being uncomfortable or nervous about making decisions, they diffuse the responsibility with the alibi "Let's form a committee."

4. Meetings represent this century's tribal gatherings. They do fulfill a deep human need for socialization, particularly for lonely persons.

5. Attendance at some meetings bestows status on those invited. While we complain about time spent in prestigious meetings, some leaders feel hurt if they are not invited.

6. The instinct to escape from their own local problems prompts some leaders to accept appointments external to their organization. Who could fault the rational-sounding statement, "I must go to our regional (or national) headquarters for a meeting"?

Are Committees Temporal or Eternal?

There are rewarding aspects to memberships on boards, commissions, and committees. Meetings bring individuals together where socializing is prevalent. Leaders hear the latest inside information. Participants gain respite from difficult or boring responsibilities. Who then has the will or the clout to kill a committee?

I was appointed to a new Experience Assessment Board in our state to review petitions for school administrator certification. After two years it was evident we had been commissioned to meet an impossible responsibility due to inadequate staffing. Yet we had enjoyed each meeting with competent friends from around the state. We relished the special treatment, which included continual coffee and snacks plus a fine lunch. Some status was involved—we were a board with significant power. Another year passed before we could gain the majority vote required to recommend that our board be dissolved.

There would be fewer committees if each had to survive on the merits of its accomplishments. Leaders should give a long hard look at whether or not their organization would be seriously hampered if some committees were killed or several committees were consolidated into one. Someone said that if there were an eleventh commandment it should read, "Thou shalt not committee."

Better-Meeting Suggestions

1. Specify the purpose of each meeting at its start. If a leader neglects this, ask "Why are we here—and how will we know when we are finished?"
   Advance agendas should be prepared which take all the mystery out of the coming meeting.
2. Distribute the agenda at least 24 hours in advance of the meeting. Indicate starting and ending times as well as who is to present each topic.
3. Identify which items on the agenda are for information, discussion, or decision.
4. Phrase agenda items as decision questions. These give more specific direction to the discussion.
5. Place high-priority items early on the agenda, when participants are more alert. Should some items need to be postponed, they will be lower-priority matters.
6. Attach essential supporting materials for agenda items. If these are more than two pages in length, include a one-page maximum summary as a cover sheet.
7. Place the following on the bottom of the agenda: "Please be prompt, come prepared, and stick to the questions on the agenda. Bring your appointment calendar."
   Since a large percentage of persons claim half their time in meetings is wasted, what can leaders do to shorten the sessions and still accomplish required business?

8. Announce that all meetings will start on time, and then be a model of punctuality. Don't repeat items of business already covered for those who come late. Doing this penalizes the prompt and rewards the tardy.

9. Limit committee size. An ideal number is between four and seven. Ten to twelve may be tolerable, though Carl Rogers claims that anything over eight is a mob. A group of 5, for example, has 20 possible communication channels; a group of 10 has 90; a group of 20 has 380; and a group of 40 has 1,560 possible communications channels. These statistics support Shanahan's Law, "The length of any meeting rises with the square of the number of people present."

10. Ask members of an active committee to reserve an hour on their calendars at a specific day and hour each week or month. Announce that if they receive no agenda at least 24 hours in advance, the meeting is cancelled.

11. Call special meetings at 11 a.m. or 4 p.m. for guaranteed brevity. Schedule "stack-up" meetings. On some Wednesday evenings in our church, one committee meets at 6:45, another at 7:30, and a third at 8:15. This allows the leader or some members to attend shorter, multiple meetings in one evening.

12. Avoid digressions. Chose a meeting monitor responsible to help the leader keep discussions on target. To keep the question or motion being discussed in mind, place it on a flipchart, chalkboard, or overhead transparency.

13. Assign items for study to a small task force of those members most qualified on a topic. Ask them to bring a recommendation for action to the next governing board meeting. This short-circuits the frequently used "let's all pool our ignorance" routine.

14. Meet where there will be no interruptions. Place a sign on the door, "Meeting in Progress." Choose round tables if at all possible. Square tables are second choice. Long rectangular tables are least conducive to effective meetings. Studies show that taking the opposite sides of issues can be encouraged by sitting on opposite sides of a long table. One wit recommends that meetings would be shortened if two inches were cut off the front legs of all chairs in the meeting room.

15. Repress excessive talkers by cutting in to quote one of the phrases and then asking another member to comment on it. A leader serving as chairperson should restrict his or her input to a sentence or two at a time. It is helpful when considering a serious question for the leader to request a "prayer minute" of silence to give time for thought before instinct moves some to "shoot from the lip."

16. Save meeting time through the use of the following notice to all members of your organization:

"I have asked _____ , _____ , and _____ to meet with me February 6 at 7 p.m. in the conference room to discuss parish education program plans and budget for the next year. Please come if you need information or want to take part in the discussion. In either event you will get a prompt written summary of the discussion and any decisions reached, together with a request for your comments."

Three or four can accomplish in an hour what a larger group may attempt in half a day—and the leader has bypassed no one who is really interested.

17. Ask each member to fill out a one-minute evaluation form at the end of the meeting.

Meeting Reaction Form

1. How do you feel about this meeting? (Check one)

_____	_____	_____	_____	_____
Poor	Fair	Acceptable	Good	Very Good

2. Its weaknesses:

3. Its strong points:

4. Other comments or suggestions:

---

18. Prepare minutes that clearly state the decision points of the meeting without unnecessary details. Place minutes on the

right three-fourths of the page. In the space to the left, place the responsible person's name next to any action item together with the expected completion date. Distribute the minutes promptly to remind busy persons of their responsibilities.

19. Remember Hendrickson's Law which says, "If a problem causes many meetings, the meetings eventually become more important than the problems." Recognizing this possibility, establish an organizational "Sunset Policy," which annually dissolves all committees. The governing board may reconstitute those committees for which there is a rational need.

20. Consider Parker's Parliamentary Principle, which suggests, "A motion to adjourn is always in order."

11. Telephone: Servant or Master?

Four of us were sitting in the leader's office. At his request we had set aside two hours to work on a knotty problem. Our group was beginning to make progress when the phone rang. Automatically the leader reached for the telephone though the caller was unknown. He talked while the rest of us sat idly by, wasting time.

It was a morale-abusing experience. At our leader's request we had reserved time on our calendars, traveled some distance for the meeting, and now he allowed an unscheduled event to disrupt our deliberations. We felt the leader's action was rude and inconsiderate. We also felt worth less than an unkown intruder.

Pavlov's dog came to mind as I sat there waiting. I recalled his dog had been taught to salivate at the sound of a bell. I also remembered how at my seminars conferees reassemble at the sound of a bell and fold into their chairs. Then I realized that when I hear a phone bell my arm automatically reaches out as I fail to consider the importance of my present task.

Frequently I ask seminar participants whether they let their phone ring at home without answering it. About 15 to 20 percent claim they do. This produces shocked looks on the faces of other participants, some of whom confess they run to answer the phone before it stops ringing.

Many of us are addicted to answer the telephone regardless of the significance of the work under way. Thoughtlessly, we grant any caller the right to interrupt us. There may be a less obvious reason for our attraction to the phone. Could its ready availability for receiving or placing calls offer a legitimate excuse to avoid some difficult or unpleasant task? Regardless of the reason, we lose our momentum and must start over again after each interruption.

This may help to explain why an international study revealed that leaders said the telephone was their second biggest time waster. It seems unreal that one of the most effective communication tools devised can also be a timewaster.

Telephones can be efficient servants—unless we allow them to be unchallenged masters. Many leaders need to develop the skill of using the phone briefly but effectively. We allow the phone to be more of a social diversion than a message machine. If our working hours seem inadequate, we will need to restrict business phone to its original purpose.

We can't denounce the telephone. It is our abuse rather than our thoughtful use that is to blame. Many of us have difficulty avoiding insitutionalized chitchat. We hesitate to terminate calls for fear of offending others. Due to mutual banter about family, weather, health, and athletic events, business phone calls can be twice as long as necessary.

Telephone Timesavers

Many of us are guilty of wasteful telephone procedures. We fail to set aside any planning time with our associates for effective methods of phone management.

1. Leaders should discuss methods of controlling phone interruptions with their office associates, paid or volunteer.
2. Leaders should resist the temptation to become overinvolved in details. Train an assistant to screen incoming calls and to answer as many questions as possible.
3. When the leader is busy, suggest the assistant respond, "I'm sorry, but he is busy now. If it is an emerengcy, I'll interrupt him," or, "He is busy now, but if it's urgent would you like me to break in?" This puts the decision to interrupt on the

caller. Most will leave a message or ask that the call be returned.

4. If in the office, some leaders feel obligated to accept all phone calls. This habit leaves no time for uninterrupted planning. Your assistant can say, "He has another commitment now," or, "He's not available but he could phone you at 4 p.m."

5. If a leader is to return a call, the secretary should record the name of the caller, phone number, and the topic to be discussed. The secretary may say, "To serve you better, could I indicate what your call is about so he will be ready to help you?"

6. Suggest that the secretary normally respond with, "*How* may I help you?" rather than, "May I help you?" Most callers respond cooperatively to such an offer to help.

7. Except for emerengcy conditions, be unavailable to incoming calls a minimum of one hour each day. Time needed for sustained planning and study is eroded when we allow phone interruptions to dominate our entire working day.

8. Group or bunch your return phone calls to later in the morning and later in the afternoon. When you have a number of calls to place at 11:15 a.m., you are less likely to spend time socializing than if you handled each call as it came in.

9. Determine which hours of the day you will take phone calls and disseminate this information. Many who call you regularly will respect your schedule and phone at your hours of availability.

10. If the secretary feels the leader could answer a caller's question quickly without losing concentration, she may say, "Let me interrupt him for just a minute and get a quick answer for you." That will satisfy the caller and prevent a lengthy interruption.

There are several helpful techniques for shortening the time dissipated in unnecessarily long phone conversations.

11. When placing a call, use the timesaving opener of, "I need help with two quick questions." Then move right into your query. Conclude the conversation with, "I appreciate your help. That's what I wanted," and terminate the call.

12. When accepting an incoming call, seek to discover in the first

minute what is wanted. Then stick to that topic until it has been covered. Close by saying, "I'm glad I could help," and conclude the call.

13. Plan your message. Before you phone, take a minute to organize your thoughts on paper. This insures prompt coverage of discussion items and prevents forgetting an important point.

14. Most ididivuals are not offended by an honest but firm concluding statement, "Thanks for your call. I do have another obligation waiting my attention."

15. Alert the other person with an advance comment, "Before we hang up I'd like to . . . ."

16. Terminate a conversation with, "If you need more information, give me a call."

17. If someone is waiting to see you, say in a voice your caller can overhear, "Come in and have a seat. I'll be through in just a minute."

18. Summarize the discussion, clarify the responsibilities each will care for, and state frankly that you have run out of time.

19. If you desperately need to get away from a long-winded conversation, you may consider hanging up on yourself during one of your comments. The other person's probable conclusion is that there has been a telephone malfunction.

There are several other telephone timesavers for leaders to consider.

20. Keep a telephone log for two weeks. This will show your peak times of incoming calls. Such information will help determine better times for planned availability and for planned unavailability regarding incoming calls. A simple phone log includes dates, times, callers, numbers, and actions.

21. Years ago I quit playing the time-consuming game "telephone tag." Previously when I phoned for someone who was not in, I left a message asking that person to return my call. Later I would find a message on my desk, "Verne returned your call." And so the cycle continued—sometimes to ridiculous extremes. Now I always ask the other person's secretary if she will help me. I have never been turned down. Then I make one more request. "If I'm not in when you call back,

please leave the information with my secretary." This procedure saves important time in both offices.

22. Use a kitchen timer to monitor your phone calls. It will discourage chitchat. Our socializing habit may result from a fear of missing something, a wish to be liked, or our own procrastination of tougher tasks. Leaders can substantially reduce the conversational fat lost through socializing without being considered antisocial.

23. Give your secretary a list of those few persons whose calls should be put through immediately.

24. Investigate the advantages of a speaker-phone which allows you to talk and do some desk work as well as involve others in your office in your conversation.

25. Except for long distance, place your own phone calls. Always give the person who answers the call your full name and whom you wish to speak to. When receiving a call, respond with your full name. For example, "This is Ken Erickson. How may I help you?"

26. Consider which will take the least amount of time—several phone calls or a memo. If you need to contact a number of persons with the same message and you wish to avoid socializing, consider preparing a duplicated memo.

27. Make an effort to return all your calls each day. Not only is it considerate on your part, but it frees your mind from any worry about neglecting a critical message.

Alexander Graham Bell's communication gift to the world is a wonderful assistant. It can become a callous master, however. Astute leaders are vigilant to see that the telephone remains a servant.

12. Problem Solving and Decision Making

"Our problem is that we need to move the outside wall of the Sunday School assembly area 15 feet to the west." Most teachers agreed with Bob's observation. Superintendent Marilyn commented, however, "Is moving that wall really the problem? It sounds more like a solution to a yet unidentified difficulty. I believe our problem is that the present assembly room won't accommodate 50 children. Aren't there other alternative solutions we should consider? For example, could we move our opening session to the upstairs social hall? Or couldn't we take out the nonbearing wall between classrooms four and five for the space we need?"

Leaders need to analyze carefully what others pose as problems. Frequently their proposal is an answer to a yet unidentified problem.

Identifying the Real Problem

One effective way of identifying and analyzing problems is through use of force-field analysis. It is a helpful tool for leaders facing an important decision. The procedure recognizes that all problems exist in a field of opposite forces as shown in figure 1. It also offers a graphic means to visualize and analyze both the

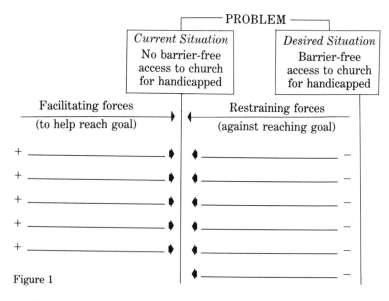

Figure 1

problem and its major influences. Facilitating forces help us move toward solving the problem. Restraining forces do the opposite— they exert pressure that keeps us from reaching our goal. The problem is simply the gap existing between the current situation and the goal or desired situation.

The problem in figure 1 can be illustrated by a church building that has no provisons for handicapped persons. Some members desire that the handicapped have barrier-free access to all church functions. The church council needs to identify the facilitating forces that can help reach that goal. These include factors such as

(+) the intent of federal legislation
(+) the leadership of the county Handicapped Association
(+) concerned members of the church's Social Ministry Committee
(+) Jesus' own commandment to "love your neighbor as you love yourself"

The council should also identify the restraining forces. These normally would include some expressed parishioner attitudes such as:

(-) "We don't have any handicapped persons in our congregation";
(-) "The cost would be tremendous for possibly just one or two persons";
(-) "The leaking roof and broken tiles in the parish hall need to be fixed first";
(-) "Our ushers could carry any handicapped person up the steps and into the church";
(-) "A ramp would spoil the aesthetic appearance of the front of our lovely church."

(The forces identified above are for illustrative purposes only and do not represent a complete force-field analysis.)

When attempting to resolve a problem using force-field analysis, the leader together with the governing board should try to identify as many facilitating and restraining forces as possible. Next, they ought to consider the following questions as helps to resolve the problem:

1. Which forces are strongest? Weakest?
2. Which forces can be most easily altered?
3. Which facilitating forces can be increased without creating counterforces?
4. Which restraining forces, if altered, would produce significant changes?
5. Can any forces be changed from restraining to facilitating?

Emphasis on increasing facilitating forces alone may prove counterproductive. Greater progress in moving toward a goal is achieved by reducing restraining forces than by increasing facilitating forces.

The primary advantages of force-field analysis is its simplicity. A secondary benefit is that it recognizes multiple rather than single causes of problems.

Decision Making

One of the highest leadership skills is the ability to make effective decisions. One of the biggest time thieves is indecision. Ambivalent individuals have difficulty becoming proficient in leadership. Competent managers are able to make necessary decisions and live with the consequences. In James 1:6-7 we read,

"Whoever doubts is like a wave in the sea that is driven and blown about by the wind. A person like that . . . [is] undecided in all he does" (TEV).

Studies reveal an interesting fact about decision making. Only one problem in seven benefits from maturing time—leaders should process most problems as they arise.

Why Some Leaders Are Indecisive

Once they reach the point of making a decision, many leaders find it comfortable to procrastinate. Failing to make a decision, however, is to make a decision by default—a decision in favor of living with whatever discomfort or problem prompted the original concern.

Indecisiveness can be related to the emotion of fear. It is natural to want to avoid making a mistake. For some leaders, perfectionism and procrastination are the twin enemies of decision making. Paralysis of analysis is reduced, however, once a leader accepts the fact that there are no riskless decisions. Problem solving deals with the future and we seldom possess all the facts. There is always the possibility of human failure, but that simply presents an opportunity for corrective action.

Leaders can elude decision making in several ways. They may waste time hoping the need for a decision will go away. Leaders also may dodge decisions by appointing committees. Too often a committee negotiates a compromise all can live with but no one likes. That is a poor substitute for facing facts forthrightly and acting on them. Also, the leader who makes a mistake learns from it and is more knowledgeable than the one who does nothing and learns nothing new.

Developing Alternative Courses of Action

Several challenges harass leaders engaged in decision making. Perfectionists, fearing a wrong decision, often drag the process on indefinitely. At the other extreme we find leaders who shoot from the hip and settle on the first solution that comes to mind.

In facing decisions, the thorough leader will consider and evelute several alternative solutions to each problem. Failure to examine various choices decreases the likelihood of finding the most effective course of action. The following process of reviewing alternatives will prove helpful whenever a significant issue is up for decision.

After identifying the real problem, ask your associates to brainstrom tentative solutions. Write these on newsprint or a chalkboard for all to review. Then determine which alternatives deserve continuing consideration by giving each participant three first- and three last-place votes. When these are tallied, it will be apparent which alternatives should be considered further.

As shown in figure 2, write the final alternatives on newsprint, identifying each with a letter of the alphabet. Ask small groups to write the major advantages to each alternative with green ink on 5 x 8-inch cards. They also will write major disadvantages on 5 x 8-inch cards with red ink.

Gather the cards and toss out duplicate items. As needed, rewrite others to combine similar points. Then post the cards under their appropriate alternatives, so the entire group may weigh and discuss their relative importance. Realize that one card may be more significant than several opposing cards. At first

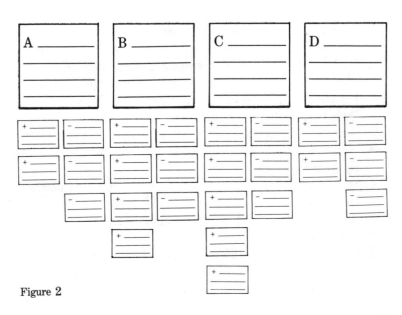

Figure 2

glance, for example, alternative "C" may *appear* to be the favored solution. Just one negative factor could rule out that alternative, however. For example, if the total cost of alternative "C" exceeded funds available by 35 percent, that alternative would prove impractical.

There is an additional benefit to this system of displaying alternatives with their pros and cons. Participants able to visualize and analyze all possibilities at one time often suggest an entirely new alternative better than any under initial consideration.

Additional Decision-making Suggestions

1. Consider carefully which alternative is most consistent with and supportive of your organization's primary mission.
2. Delegate authority for decision making to the lowest possible level consistent with reasonable judgment and availability of facts.
3. Recognize that there are no riskless decisions. The unknowns implicit in any decision make some risking inevitable.
4. Leaders can't always wait for utopian conditions before acting. Often they must analyze and decide on the basis of the facts currently available.
5. Research indicates that procrastinating with a problem usually fails to improve the quality of the ultimate decision.
6. Divide your decisions into two categories: "high cost to fix" and "low cost to fix." "High cost" refers not just to money but also to time, personnel, and effect on individuals. Waste little time on "low cost" decisions.
7. After a decision, tie down all responsibilities. There should be no question as to who is responsible for what specific action by what date.
8. If co-workers are indecisive and are holding up a decision, circulate a memo such as, "I will move ahead with the decision listed below unless I hear from you to the contrary by Thursday, February 21st."
9. Specify that your decisions are not carved in stone. They are always subject to modification as new facts come to light. Decisions remain in effect only until modified.

10. Value disagreement in the decision-making process. It stimulates imagination and provides alternatives for consideration. Reasoned dissent often safeguards us from collective errors. Many of today's majority opinions were at one time minority opinions.

Summary

Rational decisions involve several basic elements:
1. Availability of appropriate individuals—preferably a small group
2. An open climate for differing opinions
3. Gathering and analyzing of pertinent facts
4. Identifying the real problem
5. Considering all restrictions affecting the solution (monetary, time, personnel, for example)
6. Reviewing major alternatives
7. Identifying the best approach following analysis of each alternative's pros and cons
8. Developing a specific action plan—who is to do what and by what date
9. Review of responsibilities prior to adjournment

13. Delegation: Key to Saving Time

*Moses answered, "I must do this
because the people come to me."
(Exodus 18:15 TEV)*

The difficulty of delegating is not new. About 1300 B.C. Moses felt he should be all things to all people. He was kept busy from morning till night settling their disputes. When his father-in-law, Jethro, arrived, he asked Moses, "What is all this that you are doing for the people? Why are you doing this all alone . . . ?" When Moses answered, "I must do this because the people come to me," Jethro responded, "You are not doing this right. You will wear yourself out . . . . This is too much for you to do alone. Now let me give you some good advice . . . . choose some capable men and appoint them as . . . leaders of thousands, hundreds, fifties, and tens. . . . That will make it easier for you, as they share your burden. If you do this . . . you will not wear yourself out." Then "Moses took Jethro's advice" (selection from Exodus 18:14-24 TEV).

Most leaders are not evaluated by what they do themselves but what they manage to get done through others. If I as a leader strive to complete all tasks myself, if I need to be needed and am always available to anyone, and if I become immersed in too many details, I may suffer from an exaggerated sense of indispensability. Leaders in service professions are notably vulnerable to this jeopardy.

Delegation is getting things done through other people. Former President Woodrow Wilson referred to it this way: "I use not only all the brains I have, but all I can borrow." At his level of leadership it is more apparent that delegation is the key to accomplishing extensive work in limited hours.

Some leaders are so plagued with busyness they find little time for delegation. If a leader has no co-workers to whom to assign tasks, he or she should recruit and train part-time volunteers (see Chapter 15).

Why Some Leaders Fail to Delegate

Personal qualms about shifting one's responsibilities to others bothers some leaders. "They're already busy." "It won't take me too long to do this myself." "They may feel that I'm taking advantage of them by asking them to do my work." Other reasons why leaders fail to delegate follow:

1. Some leaders feel it is a sign of weakness to ask for help.
2. Other leaders are bothered by a parental type that admonishes them, "If you want something done right, do it yourself."
3. We lack confidence in co-workers who we feel may not do the job as well or as fast.
4. We have no paid employees to whom to delegate. In a study of school volunteers, however, teachers can transfer 21 percent of their time from routine functions to critical teaching functions when using volunteers.
5. In spite of the fact that all humans make mistakes, some leaders feel driven to produce error-free work—to be perfectionists. We should seek capable helpers but be willing to leave perfection to God.
6. The leader is so enamored with fighting brush fires and handling crises he can pay minimal attention to the organization's mission and objectives.
7. The leader has strong personal needs for control, power, and authority.

8. The leader has illusions of indispensability bordering on omnipotence. I have paraphrased a poem, "The Indispensable Person," which speaks to this. The author is unknown.

The Indispensable Person

Sometime when you're feeling important,
Sometime when your ego's in bloom,
Sometime when you take it for granted
That you're the best qualified in the room.

Sometime when you think that your going
Would leave an unfillable hole,
Just follow this simple direction
And see how it humbles your soul.

Take a bucket and fill it with water.
Put your hand in it up to the wrist.
Take it out and the hole that's remaining
Is a measure of how you'll be missed.

You may splash all you wish as you enter.
You may stir up the water galore,
But stop—and in just a minute
It looks much the same as before.

Now the moral of this little lesson
Is to try to improve and not worsen.
Be proud of yourself, but remember—
There is no indispensable person.

The central thought within the poem is captured in one question: "Who will take care of the world after I'm gone?"

Delegation: More than a Timesaver

Delegation is not the instant timesaver that some leaders anticipate. It is first necessary for a leader to invest some time in training co-workers before trusting them with greater responsibility. Yet, the advantages of delegation are many:
1. Expands what one person can accomplish and releases time for more important leadership functions;

2. Develops associates; helps them grow in ability, effectiveness, and self-confidence;
3. Allows decisions to be made closer to where actual problems are located;
4. Attracts those capable employees or volunteers who prefer a challenging assignment;
5. Saves leaders from the excessive cost of being immersed in operational details. (Managers should spend their time at the highest possible hourly rate.)

John Wooden, legendary UCLA basketball coach, summarized these thoughts when he said, "Why can't we realize that it only weakens those we want to help when we do things for them that they could be doing for themselves?"

Delegation Guidelines

Leaders usually have a choice of several responses to emergency problems. Normally the temptation is to gain good will by becoming involved regardless of the significance of a situaton. The concept of a "limited response" is difficult to adopt by leaders whose calling in life is to help others.

Helpful suggestions for leaders interested in delegation include the following:
1. Realize that delegation involves teaching others to perform some of your duties. It is not simple to be a patient teacher. You also may find it difficult to let loose of some favorite but time-consuming tasks. In the long run, however, transferring these to others can be a leader's greatest time saver.
2. Delegate in terms of results needed—not methods or techniques. Challenge others to discover better approaches to the mission of the organization.
3. Share organizational information fully and promptly so others are knowledgeable enough to understand and complete delegated tasks.
4. Invest time studying strengths and discovering the special abilities of your work associates. Some who appear shy may have had their talents overlooked mainly because no one ever expressed real confidence in them.
5. Start new individuals on smaller projects which will guar-

antee success. Continually challenge them with greater responsibilities.

6. Find persons who view each new assignment as an opportunity. Seek those who are capable of special responsibilities and ask each, "Are you interested in taking on a new challenge?"

7. Accept mistakes from staff members or volunteers. In fact, tell them that you expect they may strike out at times, though you look for a good overall batting average. Otherwise, fear of making mistakes may keep them from accepting any new task.

8. Let delegates tell you when they expect to complete a new assignment. Usually they will allow themselves less time than the leader would have given them.

9. Utilize management by exception with your delegates. Acquaint them with their boundaries (job objectives, budget allocation, policies, laws, contract provisions, and so forth) within which they are free to operate. Then they need come to you only when an exception is needed. This establishes certain delegated areas where the leader has "no need to know" and can avoid meddling with minutiae.

10. Use multicopy memo paper when delegating assignments in writing. The leader's copy should include a circled followup date. Ask the secretary to place that copy in the pending file, returning it to your desk on the date circled.

11. Delegate ever-increasing responsibilities to co-workers with the clear understanding they are responsible to tell you whenever they become overloaded. Reviewing their major tasks with them at that time, a leader can set new priorities in connection with their responsibilities, indicating which may be dropped or postponed as new tasks are assigned.

12. Share appreciation, credit, and recognition for work well done. Be generous with praise.

13. Delegate "figurehead roles" to capable people whenever possible. These include a leader's attendance at lengthy meetings, banquets, and conferences for purposes of an opening prayer or brief devotion.

14. Test the degree each month to which you delegate by asking

yourself the question, "What more would I delegate in the next few days were I leaving soon for two months in Europe?"

The Trap of Reverse Delegation

Some leaders unconsciously encourage upward or reverse delegation by allowing work assisttants to become dependent on them for answers. Management authority Bill Oncken says that those who come to a leader with a problem have a monkey on their back. When the dialog between the two individuals breaks off, the one who is to make the next move now carries the monkey. Leaders who wish to avoid being compulsive "monkey picker-uppers" should be certain that the monkey is still attached to the co-workers as the conversation ends.

Other suggestions to help leaders avoid becoming victims of up-bucking follow.

1. Be particularly cautious whenever hearing the approach, "*We've* got a problem." It is helpful to respond, "I'm not sure that I have a problem. Tell me about yours and I'll determine whether I have one or not."
2. Analyze incoming letters and memos. Remarks such as, "When can I have your approval?" or, "I think we're going to have to start some planning to prevent some of this break-age," both bring another monkey for the leader to handle.
3. Warren Bennis, organizational development consultant working in his cluttered office after midnight, realized he was the victim of the old Army game of "Let's push the tough ones up!" Because there is a natural tendency for some work-ers to push the toughies up, the alert leader will keep the ball in the assistant's court—for his own good and for the co-worker's growth opportunity.
4. Resist making decisions for all those who come to you with problems. Ask instead, "What alternatives have you consid-ered?" and, "What action do you recommend?"
5. Remember what Lee Newcomer, president of La Verne Col-lege, told his associates: "Don't come to me with your prob-lems. I have enough of my own. Come to me with your alternative solutions."

6. Encourage assistants and volunteers to work their way up the responsibility ladder
   a. from acting only on orders
   b. to making suggestions or recommendations,
   c. to planning and then getting the leader's approval,
   d. to preparing action but notifying the leader first,
   e. to acting first and notifying the leader later, and
   f. to acting entirely on their own with their delegated responsibilities.

Summary of Delegation Benefits

Delegation is an excellent instrument for effective time management. Supervisors need to give instructions clearly so their associates know exactly what is expected. Leaders should carefully pick the right person for each job. Also, be certain each person is working neither above nor below his or her potential. Keep the lines of communication continually open. Encourage two-way communication. Leaders can foster worker self-confidence and reinforce a desire to continue their service by prompt appreciation for each completed task.

The major benefits of delegation can be summarized as
1. allowing more time for a leader's planning, study, and creativity;
2. encouraging co-worker training and development;
3. increasing worker challenge and motivation;
4. multiplying the total service time devoted to the organization's basic mission;
5. offering genuine worker satisfaction and greater self-esteem.

14. Secretaries: Leadership Team Members

Always treat others as you
would like them to treat you.
(Matthew 7:12 NEB)

One day on the University of Oregon campus I stopped in an office to talk with the chairman of another department. His secretary reported that he was out. I requested an appointment to see him at 10 o'clock the next morning. She replied, "I'd like to help you but I'm unable to schedule an appointment." Surprised at her response, I inquired, "Why can't you make an appointment for me?" Obviously embarrassed by her predicament, she responded, "I can't do that because he keeps his own appointment book."

Whether full-time, part-time, or volunteer, most secretaries have far more ability than many leaders perceive and utilize. We need to break the degrading stereotype of a secretary as one who just answers the phone, takes dictation, types, and files.

John Casteel tells of a church secretary in New York where he served as pastor during World War II. "Mildred," he reports, "was a minister in that church." Casteel believes the primary image we all need for a church secretary is that of being one of its ministers. In addition to some acquaintance with liturgical and

Biblical matters, it would be helpful if a secretary had some familiarity with counseling principles so she could recognize special needs and even give emergency first aid when necessary. While persons with such qualifications may be scarce, they are worth seeking or training.

A good secretary, if allowed to assist, can double a leader's effectiveness.

The Leader and Secretary as a Team

A capable secretary often is the greatest underutilized resource available to a leader. A functioning team requires that leaders overcome the outdated attitude that keeps secretaries from assuming significant office responsibilities. If a secretary is really an office team member, he or she will be handling many questions that the leader never needs to hear at all.

The leader will be well served if he thoroughly checks the qualifications of each secretary applicant before selecting one to join the team. Then he should regularly ask the secretary for ideas, criticisms, suggestions, and opinions regarding ways to improve the work. Office staff members will feel an important part of the team when leaders keep them informed about all activities, ask them to meet with the leader daily, and encourage them to handle as much of the important work in the office as possible.

Many secretaries still complain that there are insufficient challenges and opportunities in their work. In one survey 85 percent of the secretaries said that the opportunity to learn new skills was very important to them. Less than half felt they had a chance for such opportunities. In addition, they resent treatment as if they were personal servants rather than persons trusted to help make decisions. As a result, some secretaries have serious concerns about the challenge of their jobs.

Secretaries' Major Timewasters

During American Secretaries Week I have led seminars in which secretaries are asked to identify both helpful and unhelpful things that their bosses do. The resulting list of timewasters for secretaries reveals problems that persist year after year:

1. Uninformed by the boss of his or her whereabouts and ignorant about a probable return time. Also being kept ignorant about recent organizational plans and revised policies.
2. Socializing by a wide variety of drop-ins. "My desk is right in the traffic pattern," said one secretary. "All the 'wanderers' catch my eye and stop to chitchat. This interrupts my work. My area becomes an informal 'social club' as visitors stack up waiting to see my boss. It's extremely distracting!"
3. Processing extra telephone calls. "Often as a secretary, I have the information a caller needs but he insists on talking to my boss. He believes no one else can help him. The total number of phone calls multiplies."
4. Interruptions by the boss while I'm trying to complete his work. As one secretary emphasized, "I wish he wouldn't continually interrupt me with problems not of immediate importance. He could make a note and wait till our scheduled meeting time to discuss several matters at one time."
5. Unclear or incomplete instructions; inadequate information. "We have no regularly scheduled communication time. I am forced to exhibit ignorance even in important areas. When asked questions others expect me to know, I feel inadequate. It's bad for morale to be forced to say, 'Don't ask me, I just work here.' "
6. Confusing and changing priorities. "When he gives me an assignment, I wish he would review his overall priorities and indicate where the new task fits into my total workload."

According to secretaries, other timewasters include procrastinating by the leader. This results in last-minute rush projects, missing his or her own appointments, and bulging files due to delays in processing material.

Undercommunication with Secretaries

In the prioritized list of secretaries' timewasters, the top six problems involved some form of communication.

A lack of regular contact between the leader and the secretary is uncaring and derogating. One secretary said, "If a leader could somehow look back into the office after 'disappearing without notice,' he would never do it again. Such thoughtlessness forces me to be ignorant where I should be knowledgeable. Not knowing where someone you work for has gone or when he may return is embarrassing. We shouldn't have to run a missing person's bureau to secure information which the leader could so easily share."

The first thing each morning a leader should spend five minutes with the secretary answering questions, sharing major tasks, and reporting on any changes in priorities. Each Friday afternoon hold a regular meeting to review activities of the past week as well as plans for the next week. At the beginning of each month, meet with the office staff and review the major objectivies for the next 22 working days.

Touching base regularly is critical to effective teamwork. It's a good time to confirm priorities, discuss goals, and clarify work assignments. It keeps all members of the team on the same wave length. Also, it's surprising how much time will be saved as callers discover that the secretary is almost as good a source of information as the leader. Time invested in communication also prevents numerous mistakes. This can save significant amounts of time otherwise wasted correcting errors.

Suggestions for Leaders

Some church leaders may have limited or no secretarial assistance. Several part-time volunteers, each trained for specific tasks, can be invaluable in such situations. (See Chapter 15 on volunteers.) Whether the office assistants are paid or volunteer, the following suggestions will prove helpful to leaders:

1. Share your weekly and daily schedules with the secretary. Invite questions for clarification of projects and of priorities.
2. Request the secretary to keep a duplicate desk calendar, which daily is matched with the leader's calendar.
3. Block out some time on your calendar which is left open to the secretary for making appointments for those who wish to see you.
4. Develop a strategy where the secretary can unobtrusively notify you when the appointment time of a visitor is over or inform you when your next appointment has arrived.
5. Provide the secretary with a current list of priority individ-

uals you will see anytime they drop in or talk with anytime they phone. Ask her to carefully screen casual drop-ins and phone calls.

6. Ask for a prioritized list of phone calls that you return at predetermined times each day. Place your own local phone calls to avoid wasting your secretary's time.

7. Alert your secretary to phone calls and visitors that you expect during the day.

8. Let the secretary take complete charge of the correspondence. Either pencil brief notes on your correspondence and let her compose replies for you or ask her to draft routine answers for you. Write your own informal short memos and notes. A photocopy can be made for the file if needed.

9. Ask that your mail be brought in at the same time each day so it cannot interrupt more important work at unexpected times. Request that the most important items be placed on the top.

10. Coach your secretary to know what mail you need to see and what you don't wish to see. Some studies show that only 13 percent of all mail delivered is of any immediate value. Junk mail is for wastebaskets, not desks.

11. Use electronic equipment for your dictation. This saves the time a secretary normally would sit in your office to receive dictation.

12. Ask questions such as, "What am I doing that gets in your way?" and, "What am I doing that you could do for me?"

13. Resist the impulse to interrupt your secretaty every time a new assignment enters your mind. Save miscellaneous items and share them during your scheduled discussion sessions.

14. Give your secretary as much of your work as she can do. Arrange for her attendance at seminars or conferences where she may improve her skills.

15. Ask the secretary to be the "guard of your time," to help you become organized, and keep you on schedule.

16. Locate your secretary's work station so that it is as free as possible from all external distractions.

In summary, don't consider this most important team member an interruption. Treat any assistant secretary as a professional associate, never as an office drudge. Build her self-esteem by challenging her with significant responsibilities. Express appreciation for her good work. Trust her as an authentic team member.

15. Volunteer Programs ___

So then, my brothers [and sisters], because of God's great mercy
to us I appeal to you: Offer yourselves as a living sacrifice to God,
dedicated to His service and pleasing to Him.
This is the true worship that you should offer.

Occasionally local congregations function without a building. At others times, congregations survive temporarily without ordained leadership. Lacking the volunteer efforts of individual members, however, the Christian church as we know it today would not exist—volunteers are those individuals who give their time and talents by choice and without monetary rewards.

This in no way depreciates our need for ordained leadership. It does highlight two facts:

1. Many Christian organizations rely heavily on the labor of love from a relatively small number of faithful volunteers.
2. Investing additional time to increase the number of volunteers and the amount of their service will prove time-effective.

In developing a volunteer program, which comes first, an individual's commitment or involvement? Evidence suggests that commitment to a church and its mission increases after an opportunity for meaningful involvement.

It's not just that the church needs volunteers. Members also need a church that can add meaning and purpose to their lives. John Casteel suggests that one of the functions of the church is to discern and liberate gifts that persons have had no opportunity to use in the world, even at the cost of a job not being done quite as efficiently. Further, in Casteel's thinking, a function of the church is to accept the skills and gifts people use in the world and give them a larger usefulness and a higher meaning than the world can give. Dedicated members *need* an opportunity to serve as lay ministers in some phase of God's work.

Feeling useful is as important for the less skillful or less competent volunteers as for the skilled. Service opportunities should be found for the physically handicapped and for those elderly that are generally inactive. An effective volunteer program, therefore, will include "passive" projects as well as "active" responsibilities. A document called "Toward the Conversion of England" proposed that the elderly and shut-ins serve in "Watchtower" groups and undertake to pray regularly and steadily for various people, causes, and needs.

A valid volunteer program will also provide some tasks that are "terminal." It is possible to recruit some people for a volunteer responsibility if it has a known ending date. Such persons are able to sign up for a short-term commitment but find it impractical to accept a task which may continue indefinitely. In fact it often is sensible to request one year commitments to ongoing tasks with reappointment possible at the volunteer's option.

Advantages of a church volunteer program:
1. Significant additional time, person-power, and talent become available to the church.
2. Life becomes enriched for those who serve.
3. The local church is able to offer both new and expanded services to its members and community.
4. Volunteers grow in self-seteem when learning new skills, when serving others.
5. Staffing needs may be partially offset through increased volunteer services.
6. Volunteers become better informed about the church at large and its mission.

Several disadvantages are typical of a volunteer program.
1. It takes time and effort to organize, recruit, train, and supervise volunteers.
2. The more volunteers the greater attention necessary to interpersonal relationships.

3. Expectations are not always satisfied if volunteer job descriptions are inadequate.
4. Volunteers may terminate their service with little notice, resulting in unexpected turnover.

The Position of Volunteer Coordinator

An individual who serves as a church coordinator of volunteers has significant service potential to the volunteers, to those served by the volunteers, and to God. Regardless of the job title (volunteer coordinator, manager, administrator, or director), the management responsibilities tend to be similar. While some coordinators are unpaid, more churches today are hiring part-time or full-time volunteer coordinators.

Competent volunteer leadership normally results in gaining the equivalent of several paid positions for the investment of one. Even if there are no overall gains in service, the increase in member involvement in church activities is a decisive benefit. The volunteer coordinatior is an enabler of human potential directed to God's work in your church.

What qualities should a congregation seek in its volunteer coodinator? This person needs to
1. accept and respect all kinds of individuals;
2. express trust and confidence in each potential or working volunteer;
3. keep all lines of communication open—be especially adept at listening;
4. be patient and remain optimistic even if some assignments are botched or incomplete;
5. earn the trust and respect of both volunteers and their supervisors;
6. have reasonably high expectations both for self and for volunteers;
7. avoid any semblance of an officious attitude;
8. have a solid understanding of the church's mission in the community and the world.

Typical duties of a volunteer coordinator include the following:
1. Develop and supervise the overall volunteer program.

2. Serve as liaison between the pastor(s) and the church volunteers.
3. Develop and keep on file an accurate description of each volunteer job.
4. Recruit and interview potential volunteers.
5. Develop a variety of tasks to meet the diversity of human skills. Select the appropriate volunteer for each vacancy. Avoid putting square pegs in round holes.
6. Organize orientation and training sessions.
7. Take responsibilitiy for informal thank-yous as well as formal opportuntiies for congregational appreciation.
8. Evaluate both the volunteer's service and growth potential.
9. Develop publicity concerning volunteer contributions.
10. Keep necessary expenditure records.

Recruitment Efforts

An attempt to recruit large numbers of volunteers with inadequate attention to detailed advance planning can be counterproductive. Satisfied volunteers are the program's best advertisement. Openness and honesty about each task and the time required not only build confidence in the program but tend to increase the volunteer's length of service.

When initiating a volunteer program it's a common mistake to concentrate on the "old faithful" members. We tend to overlook many who may be shy about volunteering though willing to serve if asked. Special thought should be given to the newly retired. Consider college students who are exploring ways to gain credit for field service. Encourage the lonely and the "hurting" to become involved in helping others. This could be one of the volunteer coordinator's more therapeutic functions.

An annual recruiting drive is inadequate for an effective volunteer program. Encourage all new members to complete a volunteer service questionnaire. Sponsor a special recruitment effort each spring in preparation for fall activities.

Announcements about the volunteer program can be made throughout the year in church bulletins, newsletters, special brochures, and posters, as well as in temple talks by the coordinator or an enthusiastic volunteer.

Job Descriptions

Potential volunteers deserve to know all they can about a responsibility before they "sign up." Most wish to feel assured that they can succeed even though a task may appear difficult. Inaccurate job descriptions may result in an unfortunate assignment to the detriment of the entire program.

An appropriate job description usually includes

1. job title;
2. a summary of tasks or job expectations—what needs to be done and when;
3. how the job serves other individuals or the church as a whole;
4. an accurate estimate of the time commitment;
5. to whom the person is responsible;
6. special skills needed, if any;
7. benefits that may accrue to the volunteer through the experience;
8. any special problems the job entails.

Don't lower the normal work standards because you are working with a volunteer staff. Capable workers take offense at double standards. The task will be a greater challenge if you set realistically high expectations. The achievement of success on important responsibilities brings greater worker satisfaction.

Interviewing Potential Volunteers

An interview is more than a friendly chat; it's a conversation with a purpose. Through an interview the coordinator seeks compatibility between the applicant's talents and the job assignment, the time demands and the applicant's availability, and the attitudes of the job supervisor and the applicant. Careless interviewing that results in a misassignment is a disservice to the applicant and to the church and its mission.

Helpful suggestions for the interview include the following:

1. If you could choose one thing that you would prefer doing for our church more than anything else, what would it be?
2. What have you enjoyed most in your previous work experience—what have you enjoyed least?
3. Of the volunteer work you have done, what has given you the greatest satisfaction?

4. Whom would you prefer to help or serve (youth, elderly, singles, shut-ins, others)?
5. How do you spend your free time?
6. Tell me about your family.
7. Describe things that tend to upset you most easily.
8. What do you like best about yourself? What would you like most to improve?

Assigning Volunteers

After the interview, assign prospects so as to make maximum use of their skills and interests. Give first-time volunteers a shorter "tryout" assignment to determine how they like the work. This will help them gain confidence in their ability to fulfill the task expectations. A trial run decreases the possibility of failure and helps insure a successful experience. Workers morale increases with the self-confidence that follows success.

When selecting job locations, limit placements to those activities where leaders are willing to accept and give guidance to volunteers. A successful program in one area eventually will do more to encourage other leaders to use volunteers than any amount of advance persuasion.

Some prospective volunteers have a broad range of abilities. Even if the coordinator believes an individual could perform some task well, honor volunteer preferences. Don't coerce persons into involuntary duties or make them feel guilty if disinterested in certain work. Also, resist judging either those who don't volunteer or those who reject a task you feel they could handle. For example, it seems logical to ask the man who lays brick professionally to serve on the Property Committee even though his first choice may be Social Ministry. Also, the volunteer who teaches school all week may prefer to serve on the Property Committee instead of the Parish Education Committee. Assignments are most effective for all when they consider the service preference of each individual volunteer.

Orientation and Training

Send a letter of welcome specifying the new volunteer's assignment as well as the place and time of an orientation session.

The meeting should help each person feel comfortable about his or her new assignment.

A panel discussion by current volunteers allows for a helpful question and answer period. Visual aids such as pictures of others at work are helpful. Consider the distribution of pertinent hand-out materials. End the session with some light refreshments.

Specific training for new assignments is best handled on the job. The supervisor should be patient and trusting. It is an important moment when the new volunteer makes a first mistake. How does the leader respond? He can quash a volunteer's self-confidence by taking over the job. Or he can see the event as a potential learning experience—an opportunity to talk over the problem and discuss how it might be better handled next time.

During the training session volunteers learn about their job objectives, whether confidentiality is needed, and the most helpful approaches to those they serve. They also verify the working hours, to whom they report, and whether they need to bring any special equipment.

Motivation

Unmotivated volunteers often become dropouts. Careless placement results in volunteers either becoming overwhelmed or finding their potential underutilized. Others may leave because they feel unappreciated, wonder if their participation is worthwhile, feel ignored, or find little opportunity for personal growth.

Well-motivated volunteers feel neither ignored nor taken for granted. They see a relationship between their work and the mission of the church. They find tasks meaningful and the service personally rewarding. Their leaders willingly answer their questions and keep them informed about the church's current plans and priorities. Resourceful leaders ask volunteers for their ideas, comments, and suggestions. Last but not least, leaders recognize good work and express regular appreciation. This motivational factor warrants further consideration.

Recognition and Appreciation

The American psychologist and philosopher William James said the deepest principle of human nature is the desire to be appreciated. The apostle Paul urged us to think about anything worthy of praise. These concepts are still important today. We are thoughtless whenever we take a volunteer's work for granted. The volunteer coordinator and other leaders can discover numerous ways to encourage and appreciate church volunteers. These include the following:

1. Encourage the writing of appreciation notes by the pastor's staff as well as the governing board president and members.
2. Mail a note of thanks to the volunteer's family for Thanksgiving Day.
3. Write a service recognition letter to the volunteer's employer.
4. Print a "Recognition Edition" of the church newsletter.
5. Plan special appreciation events for the volunteers. These could include an annual extravaganza, a theater party, a picnic, or a public reception.
6. Award certificates of appreciation designed to accommodate additional gold seals for each year of service.
7. Share newsworthy items with the media.
8. Listen carefully to the ideas and recommendations of volunteers.
9. Provide increasingly challenging work; put some volunteers in charge of projects; ask others to train new volunteers.
10. Consider selecting a "Volunteer of the Month" with a bulletin board poster and a story in the newsletter.
11. Develop a plaque for the outstanding volunteer of the year.
12. Recommend capable volunteers to prospective employers.
13. Encourage the planning of surprise events by those who benefit from volunteer services.
14. Remember volunteers with birthday cards.
15. Let them know they are missed when absent.
16. Be generous with your smiles and spoken thank-yous.

While recognition is important, it is never the major reason for volunteering one's service. We all need to feel useful. Most of us have an innate desire to help others. We want our life to have purpose. We find authentic meaning for our lives in ministering to others.

The volunteer coordinator has a tremendous opportunity to

help church members fulfill this basic life need. Paul may have been thinking about volunteers when he said, "So then, as we have opportunity, let us do good to all men [and women], especially to those who are of the household of faith" (Galatians 6:10 RSV).

A Bill of Volunteer Rights and Responsibilities

Every volunteer has
1. the right to be treated as a co-worker—as one who belongs and is needed, not just free help;
2. the right to a suitable assignment with consideration for personal preference, temperament, and experience;
3. the right to know as much about the church as possible. Otherwise, what they are not up on, they may be down on;
4. the right to feel that what they are doing has real purpose, that it contributes to a more abundant life for the people of God;
5. the right to helpful direction, including training for greater responsibility;
6. the right to willingly shared guidance by someone who is well-informed and patient;
7. the right to a place to work that is orderly and worthy of the job to be done;
8. the right to a variety of experiences if desired—by transferring from one activity to another or by advancement to more challenging assignments;
9. the right to be listened to and to have respect shown for one's opinions and suggestions;
10. the right to appreciation whenever it is due, through day-by-day expressions of thanks as well as more formal means of recognition.

(Adapted from "Relationships, Rights and Responsibilities" (ARC 2359), published by the Office of Volunteers, American National Red Cross. Originally created by Mrs. Richard L. Sloss, ca. 1960, under the title "Bill of Rights for Volunteers.")

16. *Appreciation and Praise* __

When you think that credit's due him,
That's the time to give it to him;
For he cannot read his tombstone
when he's gone.
(Edith Noll)

Bob has been like a brother to me. Whenever I drive through his town, I stop to visit him. He has the reputation of being one of the best physical-plant directors in the state. I have always admired Bob and his family.

On a recent visit our discussion centered on his work. I sensed that he was frustrated. Finally Bob summed up his feelings in a few sentences: "This has got to be one of the loneliest, out of the way, difficult, and unappreciated jobs around! It's only at the end of the month when an envelope comes to me with my name on a piece of paper that anyone seems to know I'm around. And I suspect the check is really made out by a computer!"

It wasn't that the job was too difficult for Bob. He'd handled tougher assignments and thrived on the challenge. But doing outstanding work for years while feeling unappreciated and even ignored is demeaning. Bob was on the job physically; emotionally and psychologically his heart was not in it.

Poorly motivated employees or volunteers may be an organization's chief waste of time. Unappreciated and ignored employees lack motivation. Most organizations tend to ignore their workers today.

The Cost of Ignoring Workers

Gratitude may be the least of the virtues,
but ingratitude is the worst of the vices.
(Rosalind Fergusson)

Many leaders rationalize their failure to appreciate and praise workers with the statement, "If I don't criticize them for any mistakes, then they know I appreciate them for what they do." That's not true. I worked diligently for 10 years in one organization before I got a letter of recognition and appreciation from my boss. It was an important message for me. I was happy to show that letter to my wife. Yet I had worked just as diligently every previous year but with no evidence that my boss appreciated my work. There's no correlation between lack of criticism and the presence of praise.

Seasoned employees doing a good job often resent being ignored. If leaders continually pay attention to problem areas only, they may soon find problems arising in unexpected places.

We have known for years that children prefer negative attention to none at all. In other words, they will pay the price of disapproval, censure, or punishment rather than feel overlooked. Psychologically, many adults are not that different from children. When leaders spend 80 percent of their time with the 20 percent of the workers who may not be pulling their share of the load, that leaves only 20 percent of the leader's time for the 80 percent who do good work. Studies show that good workers who are ignored tend to regress and become average workers. About 2,300 years ago Plato said, "What is honored in a country will be cultivated there." Conversely, what we fail to honor, we fail to cultivate.

Negative Attitudes

Deeply ingrained in human nature is a natural inclination to depreciate rather than appreciate. Many leaders ignore their associates until they see them doing something wrong—then they spring into action. This may be a conditioned trait learned from parents who raised their children the same way. Regardless of the cause, low morale and feelings of hostility result. Chastised workers also are hesistant to accept new work assignments. They fear a leader's criticism should they make any mistakes.

Many leaders have an inadequate vocabulary of positive words and phrases but an overadequate vocabulary to express negative thoughts. It seems natural for them to see the cup as half empty rather than half full.

Affirmative Attitudes

Leo Bustad is dean emeritus of the College of Veterinary Medicine at Washington State University. His past experience includes working with and studying thousands of beagle dogs. Bustad claims that human beings can learn a great deal about positive reinforcement from mother dogs. When raising their pups, they give nine gentlings to each growl or nip. Watching some parents, I believe that the human ratio at its best might be a maximum of one gentling to nine "gotchas" (caught for doing something wrong). There is an emphasis in some schools today on catching children doing something right—rather than wrong. Church leaders can rejoice in this trend, which is consistent with Paul's suggestion in Philippians 4:8: "Whatsoever things are of good report . . . if there be any praise, think on these things."

A convincing study on appreciation was completed in 1946 and repeated in 1979. A variety of workers was asked to rank order 10 conditions of employment, one of which was "Appreciation for good work." Their supervisors also were to rank order the 10 conditions, but as they thought workers would rank them. Employees ranked "Appreciation for good work" either first or second in importance. Supervisors, however, both in 1946 and 1979 thought workers would rank it eighth in importance. It's surprising that leaders could be so in error in assessing workers' feelings. It's amazing that no improvement in their perception is apparent during the 33 intervening years.

Those who have expressed sincere appreciations to me in the past have served as positive models for my guidance. Learning from them, I have written numerous notes of appreciation to employees, co-workers, volunteers, public officials, and friends. Some have responded and shared how meaningful these comments have been in their lives. A dear friend with significant church leadership responsibilities wrote, "When the bottom fell out of our organization's plans recently, I felt so low that I pulled your last Thanksgiving letter out of my file and reread it for support and stability."

On another occasion I wrote a note of appreciation to a former employer, now retired, thanking him for the confidence he expressed in me at the time of employment. I had enjoyed my work immensely. Later he made a special trip to see me, brought the note with him, and with tears welling in his eyes said, "Your note's the nicest thing that has happened to me all year!"

At a recent church council retreat we made lists of members who serve faithfully as servants of the Servant—the ones we take for granted rather than with gratitude. When the list was complete, we passed it around the group. Each council member took several names. We agreed to write notes stating that the council in official session recognized and appreciated the faithful service of that special member. Several days later I received a phone call from one I had contacted. His comments included, "You have no idea how much that letter means to me—how good it makes me feel. And to think that the council would take time to appreciate what I have done! I love my church and always want to help, but this makes me want to do even more."

There is a second option to writing appreciation notes that I have utilized in recent years. It stems from the saying, "If you don't like what I do, tell me. If you like what I do, tell my boss." A single example will clarify its value.

When my wife was entering the hospital for surgery, the admitting clerk handled the responsibility very effectively, putting my wife at ease in the process. Knowing how sensitive the admission procedure is, I noted the clerk's name. Later I wrote to the hospital administrator, telling of her competent service. Two weeks later I received a nice note from the admitting clerk. She commented, "Thank you for your thoughtful letter." She continued, "What you don't know is that my husband is an invalid in a wheelchair. I'm the sole support of our family. I had worked on on the housekeeping crew for years, and just received a promotion to the admitting office." Had I sent the appreciation note to her, she could not route it up the organization. Starting where it did, several superiors also could rejoice in her good work.

While able to express some appreciations to strangers, we often ignore and take for granted the contributions of those nearest and dearest to us. We may share generous words of approval with a waitress or waiter we've never met before. We may even ask that they share our compliments for the good food with the chef. But do we give anything that approaches equivalent appreciation for the conscientious work of loved ones at home who prepare and serve from 750 to 1,000 meals each year?

Few of us enjoy judgment or criticism. Jesus not only understands our feelings in this regard—He bans the practice, saying, "Don't criticise people" (Matthew 7:1 Phillips). Most of us enjoy recognition and appreciation. Jesus also understands this need and commissions us to "always treat others as you would like them to treat you" (Matthew 7:12 NEB).

All people need affirmation and appreciation in the roles they play—in the work they do. When did you last express deserved appreciation to pastors, employees, volunteers, loved ones? Face-to-face or telephoned expressions of thanks are valued. Yet you can give more thoughtful attention to written notes. Often they are kept and treasured for years. Your words of praise could be the straw that keeps a disconsolate soul afloat. And you cannot do a kindness too soon, as you never know how soon it will be too late.

17. Summary ─────

Time is a leader's most valued asset. It is the most precious resource leaders possess. While few claim they have enough time, each leader has all there is—168 hours a week. How effectively leaders use their time is a matter of personal choice.

Leading Time-Management Challenges

I have asked hundreds of participants in my time-management seminars to identify their most troublesome problems with time. The following topics are ranked in order of frequency:

1. Procrastinating difficult or unpleasant tasks.
2. Failing to plan—not placing own name on daily schedule for planning hour.
3. Tollerating all interruptions, self-interrupting.
4. Allowing phone to be a master rather than a servant.
5. Failing to keep a time audit—being ignorant of how time is being spent.
6. Having difficulty saying no.
7. Allowing discussions to wander—both face-to-face and on the phone.

Altering time habits is difficult and requires rigorous self-discipline. Few leaders make immediate and dramatic turnabouts in behavior. Poor time habits can be weakened, however, and with conscious effort, better ones developed.

All principles will not fit every person as each leader has a unique work setting. Conscientious leaders who are determined to improve their management of time, however, can identify their own objectives and work toward desired growth.

Summary Suggestions—Effective Time Management

1. Define, put in writing, and disseminate your organization's long-range mission and current objectives. Avoid being just activity oriented; become results oriented.

2. Plan tomorrow's tasks today. Recognize that planning is hard work but it's where leadership begins. Spend one day a month out of the office for thinking and planning.

3. Establish your priorities. Stick with these priority decisions. Realize that doing the *right* job right is more important than doing a random job right.

4. Eradicate ignorance of how you spend your time. Keep a time log periodically to analyze your time use and abuse—and to plan improvements.

5. Selectively neglect less essential tasks. Learn to say no to requests for blocks of time not consistent with the organization's basic mission.

6. Remember that urgent tasks often are not important and that important tasks normally won't impress you as being urgent. Problem-oriented leaders who overrespond to crises do so to the detriment of their major mission.

7. Be simple, be brief, and get right to the point when communicating. Give clear instructions. Listen carefully. Learn to say a warm, timely good-bye.

8. Confine telephone calls to necessary business. Avoid inconsequential chitchat by commenting early in conversations, "Please tell me specifically what I can do to help you."

9. Expect no riskless decisions. A leader who is making no mistakes can't be attempting much that is worthwhile.

10. Start on any small portion of a project you have been postponing. Sustain your momentum and you will overcome procrastination.

11. Jettison any feeling of personal indispensability. Delegate significant responsibilities to others and help them grow in initiative, competence, and confidence. Resist reverse delegation, which overburdens you and cripples the growth potential in others.

12. Analyze the physical arrangements in your working area. Eliminate every possible time-wasting interruption by repositioning desks, files, partitions, or other furniture.
13. Establish a quiet hour in each work day. Time for uninterrupted concentration on important tasks can be the leader's greatest time gainer.
14. Realize that an individual's personal energy level varies throughout the day. Schedule high-priority tasks during your prime time.
15. Recognize indecision for what it is—a decision in favor of the status quo. Decide what is important and do it promptly. Decide what is unimportant and decline to get involved.
16. Avoid the trap of paper fondling and stacking. Develop the art of wastebasketry—an excellent tool for better time management.
17. Strive to make the first hour of each workday productive. Interruptions are a way of life, but leaders can control many of them with a closed office door.
18. Study your co-workers' abilities. Train them in tasks you do well. Trust them with work you enjoy doing. Overcome perfectionism, which thwarts a leader's productivity and stifles any inclination to delegate.
19. Confer on a regularly scheduled basis with your secretary and other work associates. Keep all informed of any changes in mission, objectives, and priorities.
20. Care enough to coach co-workers to become as successful as possible. Compliment them for conscientious, reliable, or improved results.

Managing Time for Prayer

Regarding our personal prayer life, many of us have far better intentions than actions. Why is this?

We never have enough time to do everything that everyone else wants us to do. Consequently, important pursuits such as prayer often get squeezed out by seemingly more urgent demands. We fail to *set aside* time for prayer when establishing our daily schedule. As a result we lack a disciplined prayer life. Though replete with good intentions, we become victims of detrimental habits, which are similar to comfortable beds; easy to get into, but hard to get out of.

Writing in the *Upper Room*, E. Paul Hovey understood this dilemna. He said, "How often we hurry into the day without our armor on—without stopping to ask God to give us wisdom and courage to face the trials we may have to meet." We assume that we will *find* time for prayer. Yet, to avoid forgetting prayer we must allocate a predetermined portion of each day for prayer and quiet-time activities or we will neglect them.

Martin Luther spent up to four hours a day in prayer. Understanding its importance he wrote, "Prayer is a powerful thing, for God has bound and tied Himself thereto. None can believe how powerful prayer is and what it is able to effect but those who learn it by experience."

It is possible for church leaders to lack this dedication to prayer's priority in a Christian life. We desire God's guidance. Yet we fail to take the time to talk with and listen to God. If our daily activities are to hallow His name, if we truly seek His kingdom, if we wish to search for His will, then as Christian leaders we cannot neglect a specified daily time for prayer. It offers an opportunity to seek God's guidance as to our priorities, to request God's blessings on all His servants, and to thank and praise His name for His continual care and unending love.

It is never enough in time management to have good intentions. Conscientious, struggling leaders can embrace God's promises, "My grace is all you need, for My power is strongest when you are weak" (2 Corinthians 12:9 TEV), and, "If any of you lacks wisdom, he should pray to God, who will give it to him" (James 1:5 TEV).

Christian leaders have always labored to gain better control of time. Such striving may have inspired the wisdom found on an old grandfather clock—"There always is enough time for those things we put first."

37 6 0